INTO HIS Presence

DEVOTIONS OF BIBLICAL ENCOURAGEMENT AND TRUTH

STEVE TROXEL

Volume 2

Into His Presence
Volume 2

Published by

God's Daily Word Ministries
PO Box 700113
San Antonio, TX 78270

http://www.gdwm.org

ISBN 0-9708531-1-4
Copyright © 2001 by God's Daily Word Ministries.

Written by Steve Troxel
Edited by Sherry Troxel

Cover Design by Al Mendenhall
Creative Vision Studio, San Antonio, Texas

Printed in Canada

The devotions in this book were selected from email messages
distributed between January and June of 2001. I pray these devotionals
will be used to encourage many people around the world to walk a closer
walk with Jesus Christ and to live each day abiding in His presence.

Steve Troxel

CONTENTS

CONTENTS

CONTENTS

GUARD THE GOOD DEPOSIT

And so we begin. Though this is a day like most others, it is the day we begin to read "Devotions of Biblical Encouragement and Truth" - messages written to help us draw closer to God. On this day, we have the opportunity to begin anew and make life changing decisions. God has opened the door to our heart and invited us to draw near. We must guard this opportunity and not allow it to fade.

2 Timothy 1:13-14

"What you heard from me, keep as the pattern of sound teaching, with faith and love in Christ Jesus. Guard the good deposit that was entrusted to you - guard it with the help of the Holy Spirit who lives in us."

Yes, it is time for a new beginning. "Forgetting what is behind and straining toward what is ahead, I press on toward the goal." (Philippians 3:13-14). It is time to let go of the past and begin to set the affections of our heart on our Heavenly Father. It is time to make changes in our schedule and adjustments in our priorities which serve to draw us closer into His presence.

God has brought each of us to where we are at this very moment. As we begin to read these devotions, consider that God has given us a desire for His Word. This is a precious gift which must be protected and nurtured. Our Heavenly Father has entrusted us with free access to Himself through prayer - and given each of us 24 hours every day to use for His glory. But if we do not actively guard these gifts, they will soon be consumed and forgotten.

Let's not allow the frustrations of the past, the pulls of the present, or the desires of the future steal the gifts entrusted to us today. As we continue our journey, seeking to draw near with all our heart, let's walk with the help of the Holy Spirit and guard the good deposit.

ACCORDING TO YOUR WILL

On the night before He was crucified, Jesus went to Gethsemane to pray. The thought of what would transpire in the next 24 hours caused Jesus to be deeply troubled: "My soul is overwhelmed with sorrow to the point of death." (Mark 14:34). Being fully God, Jesus knew exactly what was about to take place and exactly why it had to occur - after all, He had set this plan in motion before the beginning of time. But being fully Man, the foreknowledge of the rejection, physical pain, and spiritual separation from the Father was nearly unbearable.

Mark 14:36

> *"'Abba, Father,' He said, 'everything is possible for You. Take this cup from Me. Yet not what I will, but what You will.'"*

Jesus cried out and asked for the plan to be changed - and yet His greater desire was that the Father's will would be done. Even with an absolute understanding of what He must endure, Jesus' sole desire was to glorify the Father. "I have brought you glory on earth by completing the work you gave me to do." (John 17:4).

This is the example we must follow all through our life - we must present ourselves to the Father prepared to serve and be completely emptied of our own desire. Only then will He fill us and accomplish His perfect will through our life.

What is the cup we have been asked to carry? Are we asking for the cup to be taken or are we yielding to the Father's will and bringing Him glory? Let's come to the table ready, willing - and empty. Heavenly Father, our life is in Your hands - let it unfold according to Your will.

FINISH THE RACE

Paul was returning to Jerusalem at the close of his third and final missionary journey. By this time in his ministry, Paul had been a Christian for nearly twenty years. Twenty years of serving Jesus, and now... "In every city the Holy Spirit warns me that prison and hardships are facing me." (Acts 20:23). Paul was returning home, but his life was not going to be easy.

Acts 20:24

"I consider my life worth nothing to me, if only I may finish the race and complete the task the Lord Jesus has given me - the task of testifying to the gospel of God's grace."

It would be several years before Paul would write: "I have learned the secret of being content in any and every situation." (Philippians 4:12); yet here, when facing certain hardship, Paul showed that he had already learned the secret.

The particular circumstances of Paul's life had become of minor importance. He knew his contentment was based on bringing glory and honor to God. His life had a wonderful purpose even in the face of great adversity and harsh conditions.

We were all created for the same purpose as Paul - we were created to bring glory and honor to God. Our specific tasks may change and be different from those around us, but we each have the same unchanging purpose. ALL we do must be done to bring Him glory and honor!

Our race is long and sometimes very difficult. We often may even wonder why we're running - but being a participant in this eternal race is infinitely more rewarding than standing on the sidelines. We must continue to run with all the strength God provides - and when our strength fades, we must run within the protection of His grace. Let's run with the motivation of bringing Him glory and honor - and let's run with a burning desire to finish the race.

DARKENED HEARTS

When God called Jeremiah to be a prophet, the people of Jerusalem had been living in sin for a very long time. It had been 300 years since the Kingdom of Israel became divided - and despite God's patient warnings, the people continued to rebel and worship other gods.

God told Jeremiah that He would no longer endure this continued rejection: "I have withdrawn My blessing, My love and My pity from this people." (Jeremiah 16:5). God also said that destruction was now certain: "I will bring an end to the sounds of joy and gladness." (Jeremiah 16:9). He then told Jeremiah how to answer their inevitable complaints.

Jeremiah 16:10-12

"When you tell these people all this and they ask you, 'Why has the Lord decreed such a great disaster against us? What wrong have we done? What sin have we committed against the Lord our God?' then say to them, 'It is because your fathers forsook Me,' declares the Lord, 'and followed other gods and served and worshiped them. They forsook Me and did not keep My law. But you have behaved more wickedly than your fathers.'"

One of the results of unrepented sin is the loss of the ability to recognize the sin. We rationalize until we can no longer see our sin as wrong. Our heart becomes cold and dark - unable to hear the conviction of the Holy Spirit: "For although they knew God, they neither glorified Him as God nor gave thanks to Him, but their thinking became futile and their foolish hearts were darkened." (Romans 1:21).

The people of Jerusalem could no longer recognize their sin - they stood before God in their wickedness and boldly asked: "What wrong have we done?" We are on the verge today of becoming equally darkened. We no longer grieve when the innocent are killed or when our Holy God is degraded. We no longer create homes which are loving sanctuaries of praise and we no longer strive for a holy life which honors God.

If our eyes were truly opened, would we be surprised to see how far we've compromised and strayed? Let's recommit our lives to holiness, purity, and worship. Let's allow His light to indwell every area of our life. Let's repent and refuse to live with darkened hearts.

INTENDED FOR GOOD

Joseph's life was filled with one difficult situation after another. By the time he was a teenager, Joseph's brothers had developed an intense hatred toward him. Their hatred led to an attempt to take his life - but rather than kill him, they sold young Joseph into slavery. (Genesis 37). As a slave, he was falsely accused of rape and thrown into jail. (Genesis 39).

It's never really explained how Joseph learned to trust God - but he did! Joseph could have become very discouraged when he became a slave - but somehow he adjusted and thrived. "The Lord was with Joseph and he prospered." (Genesis 39:2). When tempted with sexual sin, Joseph could have rebelled - but he kept himself pure because he did not want to "sin against God." (Genesis 39:9).

Even after spending several years in jail, Joseph continued to trust God when he was asked to interpret Pharaoh's dreams. Rather than take credit for himself, Joseph risked his freedom and rightly gave all the glory and praise to God: "I cannot do it, but God will give Pharaoh the answer he desires." (Genesis 41:16).

Joseph was granted much more than his freedom. He was placed in charge of the entire land of Egypt during a great famine. He was also reunited with his family and able to keep them from certain starvation. When his brothers asked forgiveness for their earlier sins, Joseph could have taken great revenge. Instead, he continued to demonstrate his understanding of how God cares for His children.

Genesis 50:19-20
"But Joseph said to them, 'Don't be afraid. Am I in the place of God? You intended to harm me, but God intended it for good to accomplish what is now being done, the saving of many lives.'"

We must all go through "dungeon" seasons in our life - seasons when life seems to take unplanned and seemingly "unfair" turns. We feel abandoned and alone. Has God forgotten us? Does He no longer care?

Joseph's life encourages us to draw near to God during the times of hardship - to continue trusting and honoring Him in all we do. We may not understand why things happen the way they do, but as we continue to love Him with all our heart, we can trust that God is in control and that our situation is truly intended for good.

AN UNKNOWN GOD

When Paul was on his second missionary journey, he came to the city of Athens which was inhabited by people who loved to worship – they worshipped every conceivable god of their day.

Acts 17:22-23
"Paul then stood up in the meeting of the Areopagus and said: 'Men of Athens! I see that in every way you are very religious. For as I walked around and looked carefully at your objects of worship, I even found an altar with this inscription: TO AN UNKNOWN GOD. Now what you worship as something unknown I am going to proclaim to you.'"

The people in Athens worshipped gods like Zeus, Hermes, and Diana. To ensure they did not overlook the worship of any god, they even worshipped a god they did not know.

Today, many of us worship such gods as Pleasure, Leisure, Entertainment, Power, and Wealth. Then as a type of insurance policy, we "worship" the Creator of the Universe. But our worship has become something we schedule and not something we live. We take part in religious activity, but have no idea how to make the Almighty God an integral part of our everyday life. We attend church services, and yet never dream of asking our Heavenly Father for guidance or direction - we attempt to worship a God we do not even know.

We ALL must ask what we really believe - and then live a life consistent with that belief. If Christ died for the forgiveness of our sins, was resurrected and now sits at the right hand of the Father making intercession on our behalf - if He will one day return and take us to be with Him for all eternity - then He certainly deserves more than our casual worship and the left-overs of our time.

Let's proclaim the truth and encourage one another to "wholeheartedly obey the form of teaching to which you were entrusted." (Romans 6:17). Let's resolve to live a consistent life - a life of sincere and faithful worship - a life lived in His presence which no longer worships an unknown God.

A COVENANT OF WORSHIP

In the message, "An Unknown God," we were encouraged to live a life consistent with what we believe - a life of sincere and faithful worship. Today, we consider the worship by the Kingdom of Judah under the leadership of King Asa.

Asa was the great-grandson of Solomon. He began his reign with ten years of peace because he "did what was right in the eyes of the Lord his God." (2 Chronicles 14:2). Asa took definite action to remove the idols and places of false worship from the country and commanded his people to "seek the Lord and to obey His commands." (2 Chronicles 14:4).

When Judah was invaded by a foreign army, Asa realized he was greatly outnumbered with little hope of victory. As he went into battle, his faith was strengthened while calling on God: "Help us, O Lord our God, for we rely on You, and in Your name we have come against this vast army. O Lord, You are our God; do not let man prevail against You." (2 Chronicles 14:11).

After God granted them victory on the battlefield, the people gathered in Jerusalem to solidify their commitment to follow God.

2 Chronicles 15:12,15

"They entered into a covenant to seek the Lord with all their heart and soul. All Judah rejoiced about the oath because they had sworn it wholeheartedly. They sought God eagerly, and He was found by them."

We all desire a more committed life - a life where His praise flows from our heart and His peace fills our soul. But we must establish priorities which allow us to spend time in His presence.

God is waiting to be found - He is longing to be found - by those who will seek Him in a committed life of worship. He even promises to help those who begin down a committed path: "For the eyes of the Lord range throughout the earth to strengthen those whose hearts are fully committed to Him." (2 Chronicles 16:9).

Our time here is very, very short. Let's not waste another day by aimlessly wandering through life - by allowing the concerns of this world choke off our relationship with God. Let's commit to seek Him with all our heart and soul - and let's make a covenant of worship.

WHO TAUGHT US TO WALK

Many events have taken place to get us where we are today. Not everyone's situation is what they would prefer, but the fact that we're reading this message says we are either trusting in God for answers or we are searching for reasons to trust Him. Each of these are indications of His miraculous grace.

As we look back on our life, we can recognize some of the events which brought us here, but many we can't - and most we have simply forgotten. God's children have always had a hard time with recognizing and remembering.

Hosea 11:3-4

"It was I {God} who taught Ephraim to walk, taking them by the arms; but they did not realize it was I who healed them. I led them with cords of human kindness, with ties of love; I lifted the yoke from their neck and bent down to feed them."

In this passage, Ephraim refers to the nation of Israel - but it's very applicable to each of us today. Whether we see His hand or not, God has been at work in our life in a mighty way. He has guided us – sometimes gently and sometimes severely - through the urgings of the Holy Spirit, through a variety of circumstances, and through the lives of many others.

None of us are at our final destination, but each of us are where we are because God loves us dearly and wants to draw us ever closer to Himself. Let's take some time to thank Him today. Thank Him for His provision, for His love, and for His promise to finish the work He's begun in our life (Philippians 1:6).

Let's also remember to thank those who God has used to shape and mold us - let's thank our pastors, teachers, family, and friends. Let's recognize and acknowledge His hand in our life. Let's always remember - it was God who taught us to walk.

STRONG IN HIS GRACE

When we are brought to the point of belief - the point where we see our sin, desire to change, and acknowledge Jesus as our only way to Heaven - we ask, in faith, for Jesus to forgive our sins and to be our Savior. At that very moment, the grace of God abounds and He picks us up as His children. "For it is by grace you have been saved, through faith – and this not from yourselves, it is the gift of God - not by works, so that no one can boast." (Ephesians 2:8-9).

The moment of Salvation is without question the most significant event in our Christian life. In fact, it is so significant that even if we stumble through every step past that point, we still have reason to rejoice with every breath - we are children of the King and will spend all eternity in His glorious Kingdom.

As we continue on this sometimes rocky journey, we are to strive for holiness and purposeful worship in our life. We are to "learn the secret of being content" (Philippians 4:12), and to "trust in the Lord with all our heart." (Proverbs 3:5). But we must also remember that "apart from Me {Jesus}, you can do NOTHING." (John 15:5). If we strive in our own strength, we are destined to fall.

2 Timothy 2:1
"You then, my son, be strong in the grace that is in Christ Jesus."

We are saved by the grace of God and we must continue to live by this same grace (Colossians 2:6). Our Heavenly Father will determine our path to holiness, purpose, contentment, and trust - and His grace will equip us with all we need for the journey.

Let's trust completely in the saving grace of Jesus! Let's apply the strength of His grace today in every trial and temptation. Let's live a life of pure and holy devotion by always remaining strong - strong in His grace.

FREE IN THE FIRE

King Nebuchadnezzar had made a large statue of gold and commanded that everyone must worship the statue whenever they heard the sound of music - they must worship...or else! "Whoever does not fall down and worship will immediately be thrown into a blazing furnace." (Daniel 3:6).

Daniel's friends, Shadrach, Meshach, and Abednego, were determined to live with an uncompromising faith. They believed God's Word and obeyed His commands: "You shall have no other gods before Me... you shall not bow down to them or worship them." (Exodus 20:3,5). These three young Jewish men took a stand and refused to worship the golden statue – their devotion to God was greater than their fear of the fire.

Nebuchadnezzar was furious and followed through on his threat. "He ordered the furnace heated seven times hotter than usual and commanded some of the strongest soldiers in his army to tie up Shadrach, Meshach and Abednego and throw them into the blazing furnace." (Daniel 3:19-20). But when Nebuchadnezzar looked inside the furnace, he was amazed by what he saw.

Daniel 3:25
"He said, 'Look! I see four men walking around in the fire, unbound and unharmed, and the fourth looks like a son of the gods.'"

As they stood before the fire, Shadrach, Meshach, and Abednego saw no chance of escape, but they placed their complete trust in God - a trust which would not falter even if they were burned. But rather than being burned by the fire, these three men were freed of their binding ropes and walked with "a son of the gods." In their time of greatest need, God comforted them and set them free.

The fires in our life WILL come. The heat will seem intense, but we must not fear - we must not abandon what we know to be true. Our faith is ALWAYS refined and made stronger by the fire. The fire ALWAYS teaches us to trust more deeply and worship more sincerely. Let's walk in bold faith, knowing He is there to comfort and protect us – knowing He will strengthen us and set us free in the fire.

THE EXAMPLE OF BARNABAS

Not even a single word of the Bible was written by Barnabas. But if not for Barnabas, it's possible most of the New Testament would not be in its current form. In the early days of the Church, Barnabas believed in the absolute best in people and encouraged them at every opportunity.

A few years after becoming a follower of Jesus, Saul (who later became known as the Apostle Paul) tried to join the believers in Jerusalem. When the disciples were not willing to accept him, it was Barnabas who comforted and defended Paul.

Acts 9:27
"But Barnabas took him and brought him to the apostles. He told them how Saul on his journey had seen the Lord and that the Lord had spoken to him, and how in Damascus he had preached fearlessly in the name of Jesus."

Paul was on fire for Jesus, but his style must have been a little abrasive. After just a short time in Jerusalem, Paul had to flee for his life back to his home in Tarsus. It's not clear what Paul did for the next several years, but there's no evidence of any involvement in ministry work. Paul's ministry is recorded again only after Barnabas found Paul and took him under his wing.

Acts 11:25-26
"Then Barnabas went to Tarsus to look for Saul {Paul}, and when he found him, he brought him to Antioch. So for a whole year Barnabas and Saul met with the church and taught great numbers of people."

Paul went on to have a greater impact in the forming of the early Church and in defining Church doctrine than any other person in history. But if not for Barnabas, Paul may not have ever preached beyond his own back yard.

We all know someone who can use a lift - someone in desperate need of a friend to believe in them - someone in need of a Barnabas. Even though we don't have his written words, we do have his example. Let's encourage others today by believing in the power of Christ working through their lives - let's encourage others according to the example of Barnabas.

SON OF ENCOURAGEMENT

After finding Paul in Tarsus and taking him to Antioch, Barnabas remained at Paul's side for several years. During this time, they taught together, traveled together, and prayed together as they encouraged the church as well as each other.

Being an encourager must have become second nature to Barnabas. Originally, his name was Joseph. But prior to even meeting Paul, the Apostles in Jerusalem had begun to call him "Barnabas (which means Son of Encouragement)." Acts 4:36. Barnabas had the ability to look at every situation through the eyes of an encourager.

Barnabas accompanied Paul on his first missionary journey where they jointly proclaimed the name of Jesus wherever they went. Another young man, named Mark, began this first missionary journey but then turned back part way through. This bothered Paul so much that when he began his second missionary trip he refused to take Mark along.

Acts 15:37-39
"Barnabas wanted to take John, also called Mark, with them, but Paul did not think it wise to take him, because he had deserted them in Pamphylia and had not continued with them in the work. They had such a sharp disagreement that they parted company. Barnabas took Mark and sailed for Cyprus."

Again, it was Barnabas who saw the potential in young Mark and encouraged him as he had done with Paul many years before. As a result, Mark matured in his ministry and continued in his service to Jesus. He later ministered alongside the Apostle Peter (2 Peter 5:13), was reunited with Paul (Colossians 4:10, Philemon 24), and later wrote the earliest account of the Gospel - the Gospel of Mark.

It's hard to imagine what form the early Church would have taken if not for the encouragement of Barnabas. We can't all stand up and preach in front of large crowds - but we all have the ability to encourage that one special person God places in our path. This world can be turned upside down (or maybe right-side up?) with each of us encouraging one another to draw closer to our Heavenly Father - with each of us sharing the love of Jesus as a Son of Encouragement.

SPIRITUAL WISDOM AND UNDERSTANDING

Paul wrote his letter to the Colossians to show that Jesus is sufficient to supply every need of the believer. In the opening verses of the letter, Paul writes that the Colossians have a reputation for great faith in Jesus Christ - their love, hope, and hunger for the Gospel was bearing fruit and growing, "since the day you heard it and understood God's grace." (Colossians 1:6).

Paul was committed to praying for an increase in their understanding.

Colossians 1:9

"We have not stopped praying for you and asking God to fill you with the knowledge of His will through all spiritual wisdom and understanding."

Paul then explains the purpose of his prayer.

Colossians 1:10-12

"We pray this in order that you may live a life worthy of the Lord and may please Him in every way: bearing fruit in every good work, growing in the knowledge of God, being strengthened with all power according to His glorious might so that you may have great endurance and patience, and joyfully giving thanks to the Father."

The purpose of Paul's prayer was for them to receive a wonderful life of blessings. But notice that Paul didn't pray specifically for the blessings - he prayed for what would cause the blessings to occur. Paul prayed for "the knowledge of His will through all spiritual wisdom and understanding" - and what followed was a life which was pleasing to God: a life which would bear fruit and be filled with endurance, patience, and thankfulness.

These same blessings are available for us today - right now – regardless of our circumstances. But we must draw nearer to our Heavenly Father - we must hunger for His Presence and an understanding of His Word.

Dear Lord, we pray that You will give us a passion for Your Word – we pray that You will fill us with the knowledge of Your will, through all spiritual wisdom and understanding.

NOTHING TOO HARD

In the 32nd Chapter of Jeremiah, God tells Jeremiah to buy a field from his cousin. This is a very unusual request. For almost 40 years, Jeremiah had been warning the people of Jerusalem to repent or face destruction by the enemy. Now the end was very near: "the king of Babylon was then besieging Jerusalem." (Jeremiah 32:2). The enemy had occupied the land all around Jerusalem - yet, God told Jeremiah to buy a field.

Jeremiah obediently purchased the field - but then he questioned God's reasoning. "See how the siege ramps are built up to take the city? Though the city will be handed over to the Babylonians, You say to me, 'Buy the field.'" (Jeremiah 32:24,25). Jeremiah had been a prophet for many years. He had been given the privilege of talking directly with God - but this just didn't make sense.

God answered Jeremiah with a simple, yet challenging question.

Jeremiah 32:27
"I am the Lord, the God of all mankind. Is anything too hard for Me?"

Yes, the enemy had invaded the land and would soon overrun the city of Jerusalem. But God's plan was for the people to one day return, "and let them live in safety - they will be My people and I will be their God." (Jeremiah 32:37-38). Jeremiah's field was a reminder that God would one day restore His people - a reminder that He could be trusted even in the face of overwhelming circumstances.

We often have a difficult time seeing how all the pieces of God's plan fit together. The enemy attacks and we don't understand why. We want to fight back, but God says to trust Him and pray - we want to solve the problem, but God says to love Him and share His love with others.

Let's put our life in His Hands and submit to His guidance - even when we may not see where we're going or how we're going to get there. And let's always remember... for God, there is NOTHING too hard!

ACTIVELY WAIT

God's Word has much to say about waiting on the Lord. In the King James version we read: "They that wait upon the Lord shall renew their strength; they shall mount up with wings as eagles; they shall run, and not be weary; and they shall walk, and not faint." (Isaiah 40:31).

This is a powerful and encouraging passage - if we wait on the Lord, we will be strengthened, soar like the eagles, and not grow weary. But what does it really mean to wait on the Lord? The Christian life is certainly not one where we "Take up the cross" and then sit down until we die. The Christian life is a wonderful journey - a journey which is sometimes difficult, but one which always contains a purpose.

1 Timothy 6:11-12

"But you, man of God, flee from all this {evil}, and pursue righteousness, godliness, faith, love, endurance and gentleness. Fight the good fight of the faith. Take hold of the eternal life to which you were called when you made your good confession in the presence of many witnesses."

Notice all the action verbs: flee, pursue, fight, take hold. This is definitely a call to actively move forward.

So, do we wait or do we flee and pursue - do we hope or do we fight and take hold? The answer is simply....yes! We are called into action - called to "bear much fruit" (John 15:8). But we are to do so while waiting and trusting God for the outcome - while remaining in the vine (John 15:4) and allowing the life of Christ to flow through us and produce fruit.

This means we are to boldly share the gospel message, but we are to wait on God for the harvest of belief. It means we are to prepare for good works through holy living, intimate prayer, and diligent study (remaining in the vine), but we are to wait on God to show us when and where to apply our gifts (bearing fruit).

God calls us to a faith of complete trust - a faith which yields action - a faith which yields patience. He calls us to a faith in which we actively wait.

BY ALL POSSIBLE MEANS

The Apostle Paul was a pillar of strength who saw the ways of God more clearly than any other individual. He had a unique boldness in his message because he was not taught the Gospel by man - "rather, I received it by revelation from Jesus Christ." (Galatians 1:12). But if Paul would have remained in this position of great strength and superior knowledge, he would never have effectively ministered to those who were weak.

1 Corinthians 9:22
"To the weak I became weak, to win the weak. I have become all things to all men so that by all possible means I might save some."

Paul was so devoted to preaching the Gospel that he could humbly minister to anyone! He was determined to reach every person God placed in his path - even if this meant becoming weak.

Becoming weak does not mean engaging in sin - God NEVER asks us to violate His commands in order to accomplish His will. Rather, becoming weak means understanding and showing compassion - it means having the "strength" to walk beside the weak and minister the love of Jesus without condemnation.

As we minister to the lost - as we touch those without Christ – there must be a single purpose to our message. Without Jesus we are ALL lost and on our way to Hell. We must never forget this basic truth. We must never allow our self-righteousness to cloud the message of the cross. The ugliness of someone's sin must never keep us from sharing the forgiveness and grace given through faith in Jesus Christ.

We each have a message to share - a message which can encourage and be used to draw others to faith in Jesus. Let's begin to share this message with ALL. Let's begin to step outside our select and "comfortable" group - outside the group we claim to understand. The Good News of Jesus is a precious, life-saving gift! Let's begin to share this gift with ALL - by ALL possible means.

PREACH THE WORD

Paul's second letter to Timothy was the last of his writings. Written while in prison and awaiting a certain death, Paul used this letter to give some final encouragement to a young preacher.

2 Timothy 4:1-2

"I give you this charge: Preach the Word; be prepared in season and out of season; correct, rebuke and encourage - with great patience and careful instruction."

Paul knew his time of ministry had come to an end - and with his last words, he told Timothy to carefully "Preach the Word." He then warned Timothy that people would not tolerate this type of solid preaching: "Instead, to suit their own desires, they will gather around them a great number of teachers to say what their itching ears want to hear." (2 Timothy 4:3).

There have always been those who distort the Gospel message – always those who remove the sufficiency of the Cross or the necessity of a repentant heart. Unfortunately, false teachers will continue to abound and will always have an audience who seek to fill their itching ears.

But we have been given a message of truth. And while this message is a wonderful blessing, it also carries an incredible responsibility. We must apply this message of holiness, grace, and love to every area of our life.... and share this message of truth with others at every opportunity.

Our time here is very, very short. We are "a mist that appears for a little while and then vanishes." (James 4:14). Some of us may vanish in a few days - others not for many years - but we will ALL vanish. What remains in the end will ONLY be that which is done for the glory of God.

Let's focus more of our time and effort on the treasures which last for eternity. Let's praise Him today - just because He is God! Let's apply the truth we have been given and share the truth with others - let's accept the charge to Preach the Word!

THE NAME OF JESUS

Jesus Christ - Creator: "Through Him all things were made." (John 1:3). Jesus Christ - Savior: "There is no other name under heaven given to men by which we must be saved." (Acts 4:12). Jesus Christ - Lord!

Philippians 2:9-11

"Therefore God exalted Him to the highest place and gave Him the name that is above every name, that at the name of Jesus every knee should bow, in heaven and on earth and under the earth, and every tongue confess that Jesus Christ is Lord."

The name of Jesus Christ is what identifies us and sets us apart as "Christians." Without Jesus there is no Christian faith - there is no eternal hope.

We know the place Jesus ought to hold in our life - but what position does He occupy in our thoughts and in our words? Are we truly on the path which recognizes our sinful condition - the path which has placed our complete trust in Jesus Christ for our Salvation - or have we allowed ourselves to remain on the path which is void of true faith? "For wide is the gate and broad is the road that leads to destruction, and many enter through it." (Matthew 7:13).

Many of our Churches today are on this broad road of destruction. This is the road which promotes great fellowship, fun youth programs, or appealing music without exalting the name of Jesus. The tragedy is that those on this road believe they are walking toward life - but they are not. "But small is the gate and narrow the road that leads to life, and only a few find it." (Matthew 7:14).

We NEED great fellowship to help us remain strong and grow. We NEED fun youth programs to help hold the interest of our children. And we NEED appealing music to help provide an unhindered path toward worship. But none of these will ever show us the narrow road to life without the solid foundation of Jesus.

Let's begin today to live a life which exalts Jesus Christ as Lord. Let's praise Him as our personal Savior in our daily conversations. And let's require that our place of worship teach the flock how to enter the gate of life - how to enter into eternal life through the name that is above every name - the name of Jesus.

GOD'S PLUMB LINE

Amos was a shepherd when God called him to prophesy to the northern kingdom of Israel and surrounding areas. God's people had strayed away and were worshiping other gods - Amos was sent to reveal their sin, call the people to repentance, warn of the coming judgement, and encourage with the promise of future restoration.

The people did not listen - so thirty years after the end of Amos' ministry (722 BC), the northern kingdom of Israel was completely destroyed by the Assyrians. God passed judgement based on His clearly presented Word.

Amos 7:7-8
"This is what He showed me: The Lord was standing by a wall that had been built true to plumb, with a plumb line in His hand. Then the Lord said, 'Look, I am setting a plumb line among my people Israel; I will spare them no longer.'"

Building a wall seems easy - we just stack one brick on top of another until the proper height and width is achieved. But without a reference (a plumb line), it's nearly impossible to determine when the wall is straight. Without a true standard as a guide, our well-intended efforts produce a jagged mess which will ultimately crumble and fall.

God used a plumb line to show that the people of Israel had once been true, but had now built their lives without a reference. They worshiped other gods and had abandoned the laws of the Lord. They would be judged according to God's unchanging standard: "I will make justice the measuring line and righteousness the plumb line." (Isaiah 28:17). On the day of judgement, all wavering will be revealed.

Our lives require a reference to call us back when we depart from God's path. This reference must be straight and true - this reference must be unchanging - this reference must be the Word of God! When we build on the foundation of Christ, God's Word ensures we will rise tall and not be found leaning to the right or left. Let's build a life which is true and does not waver - let's live by His Word and build according to God's plumb line.

THE LIVING WORD

The Word of God holds the answer to every problem we have ever confronted - and every problem we may face in the future. This is much more than standard biblical rhetoric, it's a fundamental truth promised by God. If we search for the answers and prayerfully reflect on the truth of God's Word, we will find that the solutions to our specific problems have been available since long before we were born.

Hebrews 4:12-13

"For the Word of God is living and active. Sharper than any double-edged sword, it penetrates even to dividing soul and spirit, joints and marrow; it judges the thoughts and attitudes of the heart. Nothing in all creation is hidden from God's sight. Everything is uncovered and laid bare before the eyes of Him to whom we must give account."

Without changing in content or meaning, the Word of God adapts to every situation. The Child of God who maintains the habit of reading and reflective study will find new insights in what appears to be the peeling back of layer upon layer of scriptural complexity. In reality, it is us who are being peeled back and laid bare by the ever present truths of His Word.

We do not "dig deeper" into the Word - the Word digs deeper into us! Scriptural truths are not revealed until our hunger is so great that we are willing to place our life on the table and allow the sword of truth to cut deep inside. Do we really desire to know God, His Word, and His Spirit? Be advised, surgery can be painful. When our chest cavity is opened, the condition of our heart is completely laid bare and judged.

But fortunately, our Doctor is a very skilled surgeon who can make our heart as new - a "clean heart" which is prepared to yield to the guidance of the Holy Spirit. The solution is always found in His presence - and He has given His Word to show us how to draw near. Let's come before the Doctor and allow our lives to be cut by the truth – to be exposed - to be penetrated and consumed by the Living Word.

REVERENCE AND AWE

Ice will turn to water at a temperature just above 0 degrees centigrade. We might consider the water to be consumed when it turns to steam at 100 degrees centigrade. Wood must be heated to a much higher temperature before it's consumed - and metal must be heated even more. I wonder how much heat is required to finally consume things like selfishness and pride?

Hebrews 12:28-29

"Therefore, since we are receiving a kingdom that cannot be shaken, let us be thankful, and so worship God acceptably with reverence and awe, for our God is a consuming fire."

When we begin to understand the Kingdom which we've inherited through Christ, we dare not enter the sanctuary with anything but pure praise and worship. Whatever else we attempt to bring is born in our flesh with a spirit of pride. We may say, "Look at what I've brought You!" - but God burns it up in His consuming fire. "But God, look at all I've done for You!" - up goes the heat and it's consumed.

Is our greatest ambition to impact the world for Christ? Is our motivation to be significant in the eyes of God? Do we strive to become a major player in the advancement of the Kingdom? Beware! Although these all sound good, they have their foundation in pride and will be consumed.

We truly can bring Him NOTHING of worth. "All our righteous acts are like filthy rags." (Isaiah 64:6). Our greatest desire - our only desire - must be to praise and worship the King. All of our striving to be obedient and produce good works - all of our "Godly" motivation and ambition - must simply flow as a direct outpouring of our worship.

This is a daily challenge - one of the more subtle battles between the Spirit and the flesh. While we must strive, we must also remember that God does not need what we produce. Our fruit does not make us more acceptable, nor do our failures cause Him to turn away. Let's allow His fire to consume EVERY selfish desire, EVERY fiber of pride - until all that remains is our love and worship...worship filled with pure reverence and awe.

SCATTER THE SEED

In the following parable, Jesus tells a story of a farmer who scatters seed onto four different types of soil.

Luke 8:5-8

"A farmer went out to sow his seed. As he was scattering the seed, some fell along the path; it was trampled on, and the birds of the air ate it up. Some fell on rock, and when it came up, the plants withered because they had no moisture. Other seed fell among thorns, which grew up with it and choked the plants. Still other seed fell on good soil. It came up and yielded a crop, a hundred times more than was sown."

Usually, this parable is considered from the aspect of the different types of soil. The farmer scatters the seed, which is the Word of God, and the different soils represent the different types of people who hear the gospel message. There is definite encouragement in these verses for us to be good, well tilled soil - ready and prepared to receive the Word of God. However, let's consider this parable from the aspect of the farmer. Notice that the farmer scatters seed on ALL types of soil.

In the days of Christ, fields were planted by casting or throwing out seed over all areas of a field. In this parable, the farmer is never criticized for waste as he throws seed on the path, in the weeds, or on the rocks. It was his job to simply scatter. Also, notice that the condition of the soil determined the yield of the crop - not the quality of the planting.

We stand as farmers, in the field of this world, with the Word of God in our hand and written on our heart. As we consider what to do with our seed, we must remember that the condition of the soil should not be our main concern. God has entrusted us with a message - and it's His desire for the message to be "scattered" to everyone!

Tilling soil, pulling weeds, and digging rocks are all important and have an appointed time - but in the field which God has placed us, the time is always right for planting seeds. Let's share God's message today. Regardless of the condition of the soil, let's begin to scatter the seed!

NEVER TRADE THE BLESSING

When Isaac was sixty years old, his wife Rebecca gave birth to twin sons. Esau was born first, followed immediately by Jacob: "with his hand grasping Esau's heal." (Genesis 25:26). Esau grew up to be a skillful hunter while Jacob stayed more around the tents with his mother.

In the days of Esau and Jacob, the firstborn son was given a special honor called the birthright. The child having the birthright received a double portion of the family inheritance as well as the eventual privilege of family leadership. The birthright could be traded, but all future birthright blessings were then lost.

Genesis 25:29-32

"Once when Jacob was cooking some stew, Esau came in from the open country, famished. He said to Jacob, 'Quick, let me have some of that red stew! I'm famished!' Jacob replied, 'First sell me your birthright.' 'Look, I am about to die,' Esau said. 'What good is the birthright to me?'"

Esau was a young man who lived "in the moment" and traded his birthright for a bowl of stew. He placed much greater value on immediate gratification than on future blessings. He exaggerated his immediate need in order to justify the future loss. The mighty hunter may have been hungry - maybe even VERY hungry - but he certainly was not about to die.

We see similar trades being made today. When a child leaves home in rebellion, they trade an honoring relationship with their parents for the perceived pleasures of immediate freedom. When a spouse pursues a relationship outside on marriage, they have traded a God-honoring union for the perceived pleasures of the flesh.

When we fail to "wait upon the Lord" and instead, make hasty decisions with a job, a move, a relationship, or a major purchase, we have traded the blessing of God's perfect will.

What bowl of stew are we trading for today? God has promised a blessing for those who believe in Jesus - those who trust in Him for the forgiveness of sin and walk daily in His light. He has promised to set us free to live a life of true peace, purpose, and contentment - and an eternal glory when we die. ALL worldly pleasures will fade away: "For what is seen is temporary, but what is unseen is eternal." (2 Corinthians 4:18). Let's live each day in His presence. Let's give Him our lives in worship - let's never trade the blessing.

STAY OFF THE ROOF

King David gave in to sexual temptation with Bathsheba and then tried to cover up his sin with lies and murder. How could someone described by God as: "A man after My own heart" (Acts 13:22), make such a bad error in judgement? Sin is very rarely the result of a single poor choice. Most often the actual sin is caused by several decisions which are outside of God's will.

2 Samuel 11:1

"In the spring, at the time when kings go off to war, David sent Joab out with the king's men and the whole Israelite army. They destroyed the Ammonites and besieged Rabbah. But David remained in Jerusalem."

David had become a little complacent about his duties. When the rest of the men were off at war, David stayed home with not much to do. He could have filled his time with prayer and study, but apparently he allowed himself to become quite restless.

2 Samuel 11:2

"One evening David got up from his bed and walked around on the roof of the palace. From the roof he saw a woman bathing. The woman was very beautiful."

David walked out on the roof and (much to his surprise?) he saw a naked woman in a bathtub! David built this palace - he knew every detail of the architecture. David knew where the bath houses were and knew the preferred times of bathing! "But each one is tempted when, by his own evil desire, he is dragged away and enticed. Then, after desire has conceived, it gives birth to sin." (James 1:14-15).

David's sin began long before he climbed into bed with Bathsheba. It began with letting down his guard of self-discipline and continued by placing himself in a compromising position.

We must all recognize our susceptibility to temptations. Many times, our way out of temptation is simply to not visit the place where we know temptation resides. Let's ask God to help open our eyes to the vulnerable areas of our life and then....let's stay off the roof!

IMPERISHABLE SEED

Salvation is infinitely more than deciding to walk by a new set of rules. We are not saved by trying extra hard to live according to God's Commandments. While this may be a noble endeavor and even lead to a more peaceful life, it will never result in the transformation which identifies us as a child of God - it will not result in eternal life.

When Jesus was talking with Nicodemus, He said: "no one can see the Kingdom of God unless he is born again." (John 3:3). Jesus goes on to say that this second birth is not of the flesh but of the Spirit. When we believe in Jesus for the forgiveness of our sins, God's grace gives us birth as a new creation: "The old has gone, the new has come!" (2 Corinthians 5:17).

Peter wrote to those who already believed in Jesus. They had been "born again" and had become "new creations" in Christ. But now they were under great persecution for their faith. Peter encouraged them (and us) to remember the eternal nature of our second birth.

1 Peter 1:23
"For you have been born again, not of perishable seed, but of imperishable, through the living and enduring Word of God."

Our first birth resulted in our physical bodies. We should praise God for these bodies and do our very best to take good care of this earthly vessel. But the simple truth is that sometime in the not too distant future, these earthly vessels are guaranteed to run down and stop functioning - we were birthed of a perishable seed. In contrast, our second birth, is of a seed which does not perish - a seed which results in eternal life.

We must never settle for a "good" life. The abundant, joy-filled, eternal life is only found through faith in Jesus Christ as our Savior. We must be born again - this time of imperishable seed.

SO WE MAY KNOW

In the message, "Imperishable Seed," Jesus told Nicodemus "no one can see the Kingdom of God unless he is born again." (John 3:3). This message presented a critical need - we must be born again. But it also generated an important question - how do we know when we have been born again?

Throughout the New Testament, being "born again" can be used interchangeably with being saved or receiving the gift of eternal life - this is also defined simply as Salvation. We are not a Christian unless we are born again. But, how do we know?

1 John 5:11-13

"God has given us eternal life, and this life is in His Son. He who has the Son has life; he who does not have the Son of God does not have life. I write these things to you who believe in the name of the Son of God so that you may know that you have eternal life."

The believers in the first century church wrestled with this same question. They had already been presented with a clear gospel message. They understood that "all have sinned" (Romans 3:23), and that "the wages of sin is death." (Romans 6:23). They understood the need to repent of their sin (Acts 3:19) and believe in the death and resurrection of Jesus (Romans 10:9) for the forgiveness of sin (Romans 3:25). John now wrote to provide assurance - to help them identify their new birth.

John provided several indicators of a life which believes in Jesus - a life which has been born again. Such a life obeys His commands (1 John 2:3) and does not continue to sin (1 John 3:9). But more than anything else, John states that a born again life is characterized by love for our brothers. "We know that we have passed from death to life, because we love our brothers. Anyone who does not love remains in death." (1 John 3:14).

These are given as "indicators" of a born again life, they do not produce such a life. If any of these are missing, we must return to the cross - we must consider again the magnitude of His love and sacrifice: "We love because He first loved us." (1 John 4:9). Let's carefully examine our life to see if our fruit is consistent with the "new creation" we are promised. Let's truly believe in the Son of God and be assured we are born again - for these things have been written so we may know.

ACTIVE LOVE

In the message, "So We May Know," we looked at some indicators of a life which has been "born again" - the main indicator being love for our brothers: "We know that we have passed from death to life, because we love our brothers." (1 John 3:14). Although loving our brothers plays no part in our Salvation, John quite forcefully states that if we are truly saved, we will love one another: "Whoever does not love does not know God." (1 John 4:8).

It's interesting to note that in the five chapters of 1 John, there are 46 uses of the word "love." If love is this important, we ought to understand what it means.

1 John 3:16-18

"This is how we know what love is: Jesus Christ laid down His life for us. And we ought to lay down our lives for our brothers. If anyone has material possessions and sees his brother in need but has no pity on him, how can the love of God be in him? Dear children, let us not love with words or tongue but with actions and in truth."

John is saying that our love for others is a direct result of the love of God within us. It's as if our love for God overflows and pours into the lives of those around us. If love is lacking, we must focus on increasing our love of God. Our love for others will then naturally increase.

John also makes it clear that a Godly love for others is not simply an emotional "feeling" or gentle and kind words. When we love God enough to understand His love for us in giving us His Son, we will be compelled to express our love through actions. Jesus loved us all the way to the cross and we are to love others in this same manner "because He first loved us." (1 John 4:19).

Our love of God is directly demonstrated by our real love for others. Jesus made this clear in His discussions of the end times: "For I was hungry and you gave Me something to eat...I was sick and you looked after Me." (Matthew 25:35,36). The people couldn't recall when they had done these things, but Jesus replied: "Whatever you did for one of the least of these brothers of mine, you did for Me." (Matthew 25:40).

Love must be an integral part of our Christian walk. Love must be directed up: "Love the Lord with ALL your heart..." (Mark 12:30), and love must be directed out to our brothers: If you love Me, "take care of My sheep." (John 21:16). Let's love as Jesus loved us - with more than mere words - let's love with an active love.

WALK HUMBLY

700 years before Jesus walked the earth, the prophet Micah wrote down words given to him by God. These words tell us what God expects from His children.

Micah 6:8

"He has showed you, O man, what is good. And what does the Lord require of you? To act justly and to love mercy and to walk humbly with your God."

God loves us so much that He gave His Son so we may have eternal life (John 3:16). When we understand the forgiveness given though faith in Jesus - when we realize the completeness of His love - it is natural for us to ask: "What do You require of me Lord?"

As we search the scriptures, both Old and New Testament, we will find no "requirements" for our Christian walk which are not summed up in the words of Micah. We must "act justly" by doing what is fair and right: "Anyone who does not do what is right is not a Child of God." (1 John 3:10). We must "love mercy" by showing compassion and forgiveness for others as well as a continual thankfulness for God's mercy toward us. "Judgement without mercy will be shown to anyone who has not been merciful." (James 2:13).

The final requirement is for us to walk humbly with our God. The basic definition of the word "humble" is: a low self-esteem - placing a low value on "self." This is not a very popular concept. But, being humble does not mean we act and feel worthless. Jesus loves us and gave His life so we may live. He believes we are extremely valuable - even worth dying for - we should believe likewise.

True humility is required for proper worship and thankfulness before God. We did NOTHING to deserve eternal life and yet we have received. This ought to produce never ending praise from our heart. Being humble also allows us to focus more on the needs of others: "Look not only to your own interests, but also to the interests of others." (Philippians 2:4).

All that we have and ALL that we are has been given to us by a loving God who created the Universe and accepted us into His Kingdom. Let's glorify Him with every step we take - and with each step, let's remember to walk humbly.

SPIRITUAL MILK

So we've trusted that God's Word is true and believed in Jesus for the forgiveness of our sins. We have received the gift of eternal life - the ticket which allows us into His Kingdom for all eternity. But now what? Most of us still have many years before we pass through those eternal gates - what do we do until then?

1 Peter 2:2-3

"Like newborn babies, crave pure spiritual milk, so that by it you may grow up in your Salvation, now that you have tasted that the Lord is good."

We who have "tasted" and believed have been birthed a new creation (2 Corinthians 5:17), born of an imperishable seed (1 Peter 1:23) - but we are still birthed as Spiritual babies. It's God's desire for all His Children to grow and mature: "to be conformed to the likeness of His Son" (Romans 8:29) - but to properly grow, we must be well nourished.

Without Spiritual food (i.e., the Word of God, prayer, and fellowship), we will remain as infants who never learn to praise - never learn to tell others of our new birth - never learn to walk in a relationship with our Father - never produce the fruit which brings Him glory.

Peter encourages us to develop, or renew, our craving for milk which is pure - Spiritual nourishment which is not watered down or compromising - milk of exceptionally high quality. The responsibility for growth is given to every believer - we must expect only the best Spiritual food. And as a hungry newborn, our craving must only be satisfied when we are completely full. Who of us expects to grow with only an occasional snack?

Satan lost the war for our soul the moment we accepted Jesus and were born anew. But let's not allow him to win the battle for our victorious and mature life. Let's crave as a newborn who isn't concerned about its surroundings nor satisfied until full. Let's develop the discipline of good "eating" habits. Let's crave with an agonizing hunger for that wholesome, nourishing, and pure Spiritual milk.

REMEMBER THE BASICS

As we continue down God's path of sanctification, "being transformed into His likeness" (2 Corinthians 3:18), moving from milk to solid food (Hebrews 5:12), and growing in grace and "all spiritual wisdom and understanding" (Colossians 1:9), it is wise to continually return to the basics of our faith. As we ponder the "deeper truths," we must never forget that "God so loved the world that He gave His one and only Son, that whoever believes in Him shall not perish but have eternal life." (John 3:16).

2 Peter 1:12-13
"So I will always remind you of these things, even though you know them and are firmly established in the truth you now have. I think it is right to refresh your memory as long as I live."

Peter knew the importance of fundamentals when he wrote these instructions to all believers. Peter wanted us to remember: "His divine power has given us everything we need for life and godliness." (2 Peter 1:3). At the moment of Salvation, we receive everything we need to live a victorious life and "escape the corruption in the world caused by evil desires." (2 Peter 1:4). Our challenge is to learn how to best utilize what we have already received.

Peter also wanted us to remember that Salvation is not our final destination - rather, it is the beginning of a long and wonderful journey. However, this journey MUST begin with faith and then grow - there are no short cuts!

2 Peter 1:5-7
"For this very reason, make every effort to add to your faith goodness; and to goodness, knowledge; and to knowledge, self-control; and to self-control, perseverance; and to perseverance, godliness; and to godliness, brotherly kindness; and to brotherly kindness, love."

To ensure we don't wander down side paths filled with self-effort and self-importance - or corruption and evil desires - let's return to the starting point of our faith and continue walking forward once again. Let's dig deep at every opportunity, but let's always remember the basics.

OUR UNCONDITIONAL LOVE

Most of us are aware of God's unconditional love. When we become His children through faith in Jesus, He loves us in spite of our failures - in spite of the way we stumble and fall. But what type of love do we give in return? Do we have a devotional love which remains through good times as well as bad, or have we unknowingly attached conditions?

The prophet Habakkuk ministered during the same general time period as Jeremiah, Daniel, and Ezekiel. This was a time when the southern kingdom of Judah was being invaded by Babylon and there was great wickedness in the land. Habakkuk asked God many of the same questions we might ask today: "How long, O Lord, must I call for help, but You do not listen? Or cry out to you, 'Violence!' but You do not save?" (Habakkuk 1:2).

Habakkuk was frustrated that God appeared slow in answering his prayer and was allowing so much evil to go unpunished. Yet through these trials, Habakkuk developed an unwavering devotion - a true love for his Heavenly Father.

Habakkuk 3:17-18
> *"Though the fig tree does not bud and there are no grapes on the vines, though the olive crop fails and the fields produce no food, though there are no sheep in the pen and no cattle in the stalls, yet I will rejoice in the Lord, I will be joyful in God my Savior."*

Habakkuk presented his concerns, but regardless of the outcome, his love for God would remain unchanged. This same love was expressed by Shadrach, Meshach and Abednego before they were thrown into the fiery furnace. They knew that God could save them, but their love did not depend on being rescued: "But even if He does not {save us}, we want you to know, O king, that we will not serve your gods or worship the image of gold you have set up." (Daniel 3:18).

There will be times when the world around us is falling apart - times when our life begins to crumble and the heat of the furnace seems very real. There will also be many times when we do not understand God's plan or timing. When this occurs, we must strive for a love that doesn't waver - a love which isn't torn apart by the forces of the wind.

Our Heavenly Father is our source of strength, "He alone is my rock and my salvation" (Psalm 62:2). Let's give Him our very best - our very best worship and devotion - let's give Him our unconditional love.

ALL HIS ENERGY

When the Apostle Paul met Jesus on the road to Damascus, his life was forever changed. Prior to meeting Jesus, Paul was "breathing out murderous threats against the Lord's disciples." (Acts 9:1). After the encounter with Jesus and being filled with the Holy Spirit, Paul "began to preach in the synagogues that Jesus is the Son of God." (Acts 9:20).

Paul had been given the task of preaching the gospel of God's grace through faith in Jesus - and he would do so for the remainder of his life. Paul endured many trials. He faced those who desired to take his life and others who simply refused to listen to his message - but Paul continued on.

Colossians 1:29

"To this end I labor, struggling with all His energy, which so powerfully works in me."

Paul "labored" and "struggled" with the task he had been given. But rather than rely on his own strength and abilities, Paul learned to labor with the energy of Jesus.

The word Paul used for "energy" refers to the working of God's strength through an individual. Paul used this same word when he wrote to the church in Ephesus: "That power is like the {energy} of His mighty strength, which He exerted in Christ when He raised Him from the dead and seated Him at the right hand in the Heavenly realms." (Ephesians 1:19-20).

God makes His strength available to those who believe. The same power that flowed through Jesus and raised Him from the dead is available to flow through us today. This is a remarkable gift - yet it's one we seldom use.

There will be times of overwhelming adversity when God will simply take charge and directly fight the enemy. But the majority of our journey will be the daily labor - the struggles to accomplish God's work.

We only grow weary when we rely on our own energy: "I can do EVERYTHING through Him who gives me strength." (Philippians 4:13). We are NEVER given more than we can handle! We can do ALL things...when we labor with all HIS energy.

A CHILDLIKE AMAZEMENT

My daughter Sarah is now four and a half years old. I have the privilege of reading to her every night before she goes to bed. This is a special time we both greatly enjoy. About a month ago we began reading through a children's story bible. Last night, we read the story of young Samuel as recorded in 1 Samuel, Chapter 3.

Samuel was ministering in the temple as a helper to an old priest named Eli. One night God called to Samuel - but Samuel thought it was Eli's voice. Eli said he didn't call and told Samuel to go back to bed. After God called a few more times, Samuel answered: "Speak, for Your servant is listening." (1 Samuel 3:10). God then gave young Samuel a message - but the message was all about Eli.

My daughter then asked, "Why did God talk to Samuel and not Eli?" We then talked about how we must be ready to hear God and WANT to hear Him. I said Eli may have had some problems in his life which kept him from hearing God - so God spoke His message through a child. I then said young children (like her) can often hear God better than old people (like me).

"But I don't hear God talk to me," she said, with a little disappointment in her voice. I explained how God doesn't usually speak so we can hear Him with our ears - rather, He speaks to our heart and then we hear Him as we listen to our heart. At that point her little eyes widened and she replied, "Like today when I was going to sit on one of the baby toys - Jesus told my heart that I was too big and shouldn't do it so I listened to what He said."

I encouraged her that this is exactly how God speaks to us - we just need to learn how to listen and then obey. My daughter thought for a moment and then slowly shook her head in amazement: "Wow! That's soooooo cool!!"

Matthew 18:3
"And He said: 'I tell you the truth, unless you change and become like little children, you will never enter the kingdom of heaven.'"

I'm quite fortunate to have the opportunity to spend time every day reading God's Word and pondering His truths. It's my prayer that I never lose the ability to look at the wonders of God and say, "Wow! That's soooooo cool!!" Thank you, Sarah, for reminding us of our need to look at God with a childlike amazement.

KNOWING CHRIST

While in prison in Rome, Paul wrote about his true desires - that which filled his life with meaning.

Philippians 3:10
"I want to know Christ and the power of His resurrection and the fellowship of sharing in His sufferings, becoming like Him in His death."

Paul knew exactly what brought him fulfillment. He passionately pursued a relationship with Jesus and sought to be identified with His death and resurrection. Paul's desire was to know Christ.

We must make a careful distinction between truly knowing Christ and simply knowing "about" Him. We can fill our head with every possible biblical fact and still never know Christ. To know Christ is to love Him and to draw intimately close to Him - close in our joy as well as our suffering. To Paul, there was nothing else in life that had any meaning: "I consider everything a loss compared to the surpassing greatness of knowing Christ Jesus my Lord." (Philippians 3:8a).

Paul's passion for Jesus would allow him to abandon everything - without hesitation: "I consider them rubbish that I may gain Christ." (Philippians 3:8b). It was this uncontested supremacy of Christ in Paul's life which led to his "being content in any and every situation." (Philippians 4:12).

We have the same ability to know Christ today - and the same promise of contentment. Our emptiness will never be filled through more possessions, more activities, or more relationships - these are all temporary and will eventually fade away. Our life will only be complete when we fully give ourselves to Jesus and love Him without reservation - we will only be filled as we endeavor to know Him.

We may never be asked to give up everything - but our heart must be prepared and ready to do so if called. Anything which we refuse to let go has effectively become our god. Let's make certain that Jesus is solidly on the throne. Let's reconsider our priorities and make sure nothing has become more important than knowing Christ.

CALLING GOD A LIAR

The Bible was written by men, but inspired and directed by the Holy Spirit. Many times, as in the case of the prophets, the words were transcribed directly from God as He spoke. Other times, the words came as a result of direct observation or Spiritual insight. The Bible was given to us by God to instruct us in how to live and to reveal to us the character and nature of our Heavenly Father. Most of us say we believe God's Word is true - but do we really act like we believe?

1 John 5:10

"Anyone who believes in the Son of God has this testimony in his heart. Anyone who does not believe God has made Him out to be a liar, because he has not believed the testimony God has given about His Son."

Yes, our old nature sometimes gets in the way and clouds our ability to clearly see the truth. Yes, some of God's truths can be hard to accept and actually put into practice. But, we either believe His words and begin to take steps to apply them in our life or we are calling God a liar.

"Well, of course I don't think God's a liar. It's just....." It's just what? It may be hard, but we must confront our beliefs and begin to make them real. When we face a trial and don't know which direction to turn, do we believe God's Word?

"Trust in the Lord with all your heart and lean not on your own understanding; in all your ways acknowledge Him, and He will make your paths straight." (Proverbs 3:5-6). Do we really believe He will make our paths straight?

"And we know that in all things God works for the good of those who love Him, who have been called according to His purpose." (Romans 8:28). Do we really believe God is working for the good in All things?

How about the promises of being content (Philippians 4:12), or being given the peace of Jesus (John 14:27), or the fruit of the Spirit (Galatians 5:22-23) - can we really "do everything through Him who gives me strength?" (Philippians 4:13). Parents, do we believe: "Train a child in the way he should go, and when he is old he will not turn from it?" (Proverbs 22:6).

God's Word is true and His promises are real! Praise Him!! Now, let our lives demonstrate that we REALLY believe - let's make sure our actions and decisions, fears and anxieties, are NOT calling God a liar.

GOD'S THERMAL

All of us have experienced a low valley where we thought the sun would never shine again. We probably wandered for a while in this gloom before something happened and we found ourselves rising to new heights.

Isaiah 40:29-31

"He gives strength to the weary and increases the power of the weak. Even youths grow tired and weary, and young men stumble and fall; but those who hope in the Lord will renew their strength. They will soar on wings like eagles; they will run and not grow weary, they will walk and not be faint."

An eagle seems to fly effortlessly through the air with only an occasional flap of the wings. These great birds are experts at finding areas of rising air called thermals which allow them to soar without using any of their own energy.

God uses Spiritual thermals to lift us up when we're down. Usually these thermals are administered through other people in the form of encouraging words or deeds. What happened the last time we were stuck in the valley? Chances are someone encouraged us and we soared.

If we find ourself back in the valley today, we must continue to hope in the Lord - to trust that our thermal is on the way. If we're currently soaring high, we must give praise and honor to our Heavenly Father - but we must also recognize there are many others in the valley who are looking for a lift.

God has chosen to use people to accomplish much of His work on earth. He could have chosen other methods - Jesus said: "If they {the people} keep quiet, the stones will cry out." (Luke 19:40) - but He chose us. We are to "encourage one another daily," (Hebrews 3:13). Why? Because there is a valley full of people waiting and hoping for that rising wind to lift them up.

We have been adopted into the "Family" of God - and our Family needs each other very much! Let's live a life of encouragement - let's live a life dedicated to being God's thermal!

NOTHING CAN COMPARE

Abraham was advancing in age (over 80 years old) and became a little frustrated with God because he didn't have any children: "You have given me no children; so a servant in my household will be my heir." (Genesis 15:3). But God had other plans and made a promise to Abraham.

Genesis 15:4-5

"Then the word of the Lord came to him: 'This man will not be your heir, but a son coming from your own body will be your heir.' He took him outside and said, 'Look up at the heavens and count the stars - if indeed you can count them.' Then He said to him, 'So shall your offspring be.'"

Abraham waited many years for God's promise to be fulfilled (he was 100 years old when Isaac was born). But God honored His promise in a way that was much better than anything Abraham could have imagined. Through Isaac, Jacob was born - and from Jacob came the 12 families who would be the beginning of the nation of Israel.

God gives us many promises today - but they all flow from the promise first stated by Jesus:

John 3:16

"For God so loved the world that He gave His one and only Son, that whoever believes in Him shall not perish but have eternal life."

Eternal life!! When we fully understand, we will know that nothing the world can offer will EVER compare to the promises of God - nothing can provide greater peace...and NOTHING else will last for all eternity. When we fully understand, perhaps we will spend less of our time and effort on pursuits with no real value.

Jesus Christ shed His blood as a sacrifice for the sin of those who believe. His sacrifice provides a way for us to have eternal life. Let's hold tightly to His promise - and let's always remember...NOTHING can compare!

HIS DEVOTED SLAVE

Not many of us consider ourselves to be a slave. We may feel as if our boss or certain family members treat us like a slave, but slavery is defined as "a person who is the legal property of and has to serve another." All right, some of us are still thinking of our boss or family. Well, in truth, God's Word says we are all slaves.

Romans 6:20-22

"When you were slaves to sin, you were free from the control of righteousness. What benefit did you reap at that time from the things you are now ashamed of? Those things result in death! But now that you have been set free from sin and have become slaves to God, the benefit you reap leads to holiness, and the result is eternal life."

Paul teaches that we are all born into slavery - we are born slaves to sin. The only way to be set free from the mastery of sin and death is to ask for a transfer of ownership and become a slave to God. Our new Master then has the grace and power to shatter the bonds of sin and give us the gift of eternal life. Notice the implication: We are never free unto ourselves - never our own masters. Many live under the illusion of freedom, but we are either a slave to sin or a slave to God.

If today finds us struggling to break the bondage of sin, then we must stop fighting! This is not a battle we can win with our own strength! The only way to be truly free is to submit ourself to God and accept the gift of forgiveness through Jesus. Without His gift, we will be forever under the control of our sinful nature.

Romans 8:5-6

"Those who live according to the sinful nature have their minds set on what that nature desires; but those who live in accordance with the Spirit have their minds set on what the Spirit desires. The mind of sinful man is death, but the mind controlled by the Spirit is life and peace."

God is sending out His call around the world today. In the stillness of our heart we've heard Him call us to a closer and more intimate relationship - a more consistent life with true devotion and praise. He is requiring us to make a choice: "Choose this day whom you will serve." (Joshua 24:15). We have been offered freedom from the power of sin and death. Let's fully embrace His gift, submit to His guidance, worship Him with all our heart, and forever become...His devoted slave.

AN UNBLEMISHED SACRIFICE

During the days of Moses, God established very specific laws for the sacrifices. God called for animal sacrifices to teach His people the seriousness of sin and to prepare the way for Jesus as the final sacrifice. God taught that when a sacrifice was offered, it was to be pure and without blemish: "If the offering is a burnt offering from the herd, he is to offer a male without defect. He must present it at the entrance to the Tent of Meeting so that it will be acceptable to the Lord." (Leviticus 1:3).

Malachi was the last prophet of the Old Testament and served approximately 800 years after the law was given to Moses. The people of Israel had gone through many highs and lows in their worship and were currently on another downward spiral. The priests had become very casual with the sacrifices; so God spoke His displeasure in an attempt to turn their hearts back toward a condition of reverence.

Malachi 1:7-8

"You place defiled food on My altar. But you ask, `How have we defiled You?' By saying that the Lord's table is contemptible. When you bring blind animals for sacrifice, is that not wrong? When you sacrifice crippled or diseased animals, is that not wrong?"

With the sacrifice of Jesus, the need for animal sacrifices has ended: "He entered the Most Holy Place once for all by His own blood." (Hebrews 9:12). Through faith in Jesus, our sins are completely forgiven.

Each of us who have experienced God's mercy and grace are now urged "to offer our bodies as a living sacrifice, holy and pleasing to God." (Romans 12:1a). We offer this sacrifice not to earn or even maintain our Salvation - we offer this sacrifice because "this is our Spiritual act of worship." (Romans 12:1b).

We are to present ourselves to God and allow Him to use us for His glory. But, we are to offer ourselves with a pure heart - a heart without selfish ambition or pride - a heart which refuses to compromise with the world - a heart without blemish.

God has given us all we have and made us all we are. Let's worship and serve Him with a pure heart - let's present our lives to Him as an unblemished sacrifice.

NEW GAME RULES

In basketball, the team with the most points at the end of the game wins. But, if we attempt to apply basketball rules to the game of golf, we will lose every time - golf is played with different rules and requires a different strategy. Needless to say, it's critical to know and understand the rules of the game in which we are competing.

Matthew 19:30
"But many who are first will be last, and many who are last will be first."

Jesus came with a message that the rules of this life are not as they may seem. The first, by the world's standard, will not necessarily win. But the one who follows Jesus is promised the victor's crown - eternal life.

When the clock of life ticks its last, it will not be the one with the biggest bank account, biggest house, or nicest car who will stand first - it won't even be the one who pastors the largest church or has led the most people to Jesus who will stand victorious. Rather, it will be the child who lives according to the priorities established by Christ.

When Jesus was asked what was the greatest commandment, He said: "Love the Lord your God with all your heart and with all your soul and with all your mind and with all your strength." (Mark 12:30). The greatest commandment must be our greatest priority and the foundation on which we build our life, our family, and our ministry.

Many of us feel like we're falling behind because of our decision to follow Christ. We see the wicked prosper and start to believe we must compromise in order to keep pace - but the game rules have changed! The world around us has the wrong uniform, wrong equipment, and wrong play book. The great deceiver would like to fill us with doubt, but we must not be swayed. The final score will be revealed on the day of judgement when we stand before our Lord.

No matter how loud the competition yells that we're going the wrong way, we must boldly continue down the path of truth. We have already won! When God gave us His Son and told us to believe, He also established...new game rules!

RUN WITH PERSEVERANCE

Our life can be a long and sometimes difficult race. But this race is not like any we have ever run before. We do not compete against the other runners - nor do we all even run the same course. We run the race marked out for us by our Heavenly Father - and yet, we ALL must strive toward the same finish line.

Hebrews 12:1-2

"Let us throw off everything that hinders and the sin that so easily entangles, and let us run with perseverance the race marked out for us. Let us fix our eyes on Jesus, the author and perfecter of our faith."

The dictionary defines perseverance as: "To persist in spite of opposition or discouragement." The writer of Hebrews is telling us to run the race - and to keep running in spite of the adversity we're sure to face. We are to throw off the things that would slow us down and continue on...with our eyes firmly fixed on Jesus.

The weeds along the side of our path often try to wrap around our legs and pull us down. This "sin that so easily entangles" can be difficult to even recognize. We may be running down a clear path without even a hint of weeds. Everything has been going well and we feel immune to the temptations of this world. But without our eyes fixed on Jesus - without our heart fully trusting Him for every step - our path can become covered and we can become completely immersed in a sea of weeds before we even know there's a problem.

The race we have been called to run is a long marathon, not a quick sprint. In order to persevere, we must prepare for many hills, valleys, and weeds along the way. We must have that burning desire in our heart to one day boldly say: "I have fought the good fight, I have finished the race, I have kept the faith." (2 Timothy 4:7).

We must not stop. No matter what weeds this day may contain, we must continue to run with our eyes firmly fixed on Jesus until we hear Him say: "well done good and faithful servant." (Matthew 25:23). Let's stay in the race! Let's run to bring Him glory and honor - and let's run with perseverance!

OUR PRIVILEGED RESPONSIBILITY

God has always set aside a select group to carry forth His Word and to help guide His people. In the Old Testament times, God designated the descendants of Levi to be priests. The priests were to perform the various sacrifices, give instruction regarding God's Law, and be the general interface between God and man. This great privilege also carried an enormous responsibility - the priests were accountable to God for maintaining His standard.

Malachi served as a prophet of God approximately 900 years after the Levitical priesthood was established. The priests once held a deep reverence for God - but they wandered away and lost all sense of their calling. Through Malachi, God sent the priests a sharp rebuke.

Malachi 2:7-9

"For the lips of a priest ought to preserve knowledge, and from his mouth men should seek instruction - because he is the messenger of the Lord Almighty. But you have turned from the way and by your teaching have caused many to stumble... you have not followed My ways."

When Jesus came to earth and gave Himself as a sacrifice for our sins, a new covenant was established. No longer would there be only a select group of priests who had access to God. Now, all believers are "a chosen people, a royal priesthood, a holy nation, a people belonging to God." (1 Peter 2:9).

The primary duty of a priest was to seek God's will and communicate the truth of God's Word to those under his care. As members of God's royal priesthood, we now have this same responsibility. We must seek His will and speak truth to those He places in our path.

Each of us has someone in our life who is seeking - seeking for someone to show them the way - seeking for someone who will reveal the truth by their actions as well as their words. Like it or not, we are that someone! We are never held accountable for the response of others - only for our presentation of the truth.

We must now be faithful to the calling of the royal priesthood. We must become a priest within our family, our work, and among our friends. We must diligently seek His will and not stray. We must learn His truths and live by them...and speak His truth in love. Let's praise Him for giving us the opportunity to serve - for allowing us to lead others to a closer relationship with our Heavenly Father - for giving us our privileged responsibility.

INCREASE THE LIGHT

In the physical world, there is no measurable quantity to define darkness. Dark is simply the absence of light and the measure of darkness can only be in reference to the measure of light - greater darkness means less light.

In the Spiritual realm, we usually associate darkness with things that are wicked or evil, and light with things that are holy or pure - darkness with the forces of Satan, and light with the forces of God. But the concept is the same - darkness only exists when a void is left by the absence of light. Light and dark can not exist at the same time - when the light is increased, the darkness automatically fades.

1 John 1:5-6
"This is the message we have heard from Him and declare to you: God is light; in Him there is no darkness at all. If we claim to have fellowship with Him yet walk in the darkness, we lie and do not live by the truth."

There is no question that the gospel message is one of Salvation by the grace of God through faith in the sacrifice of Jesus and not through anything we do. (Ephesians 2:8-9). But once we are saved, we begin an eternal fellowship with Jesus Christ - the true and eternal Light. It is not possible for us to have fellowship with the Light and still live a life filled with darkness.

When a life IS filled with darkness, we need to understand: it doesn't make sense to talk about the removal of darkness - only the addition or increase of Light. By focusing on the darkness, we clean only the outside but leave the heart dark and dead - we must focus all effort on the Light of Jesus. "First clean the inside of the cup and dish, and then the outside also will be clean." (Matthew 23:26).

We should also remember that in total darkness, there are no distinguishing features - good appears the same as evil. Without the Light, we generally waste our time by attempting to point out evil - a person in total darkness cannot even recognize evil. Only by first receiving the Light will the evil be exposed and begin to fade.

God has "saved us and called us to a holy life," (2 Timothy 1:9); called us to a life filled with Light. If our Spiritual life becomes dim, we must focus on the only sure way to remove darkness - we must increase the Light.

A FAMINE OF HEARING

Like most of the Old Testament prophets, Amos was chosen by God to deliver a message of repentance. The people of Israel had wandered away from God and now showed little interest in returning to a life of worship. The economy was thriving and the people had very few unmet needs. Therefore, they paid no attention to the messages delivered by Amos.

Through Amos, God sent a strong warning. Although He promises to answer all those who respond to His call - and promises to be VERY patient - He also warns that the opportunity to hear may not always be available.

Amos 8:11-12

> *"'The days are coming,' declares the Sovereign Lord, 'when I will send a famine through the land - not a famine of food or a thirst for water, but a famine of hearing the words of the Lord. Men will stagger from sea to sea and wander from north to east, searching for the word of the Lord, but they will not find it.'"*

When we hear the Word of God, the door is open and we are in the middle of a God-directed opportunity. When we reject His Word, we begin to close the door and harden our heart - the opportunity fades: "So, as the Holy Spirit says: 'Today, if you hear His voice, do not harden your hearts.'" (Hebrews 3:7-8).

We have been blessed to live during this time in history. Yes, we are faced with the unrelenting pressures of an over-indulgent, self-consumed society - but we have also been blessed with a wonderful abundance of the Word of God. Those who are searching need not look far to find the truth. We have many opportunities to hear the Word and to grow in grace and knowledge.

Our Heavenly Father loves us dearly. He "wants ALL men to be saved," (1 Timothy 2:4) - and wants all who are saved to be "conformed to the likeness of His Son." (Romans 8:29). He is calling us today - calling us to know Him with a greater and more intimate love. Let's listen to His Words - let's make good use of this opportunity and praise Him that we do not live during a famine of hearing.

KNOWN BY OUR LOVE

The Church in Ephesus was established by the Apostle Paul and became one of the most prominent churches in the early days of Christianity. Paul ministered in Ephesus for three years (Acts 19:1-20), and a few years later, wrote them a special letter of encouragement - the book of Ephesians.

The Ephesians were doing most things "right." They had strong programs and a work ethic which should characterize any thriving church: "I {Jesus} know your deeds, your hard work and your perseverance. I know that you cannot tolerate wicked men, that you have tested those who claim to be apostles but are not, and have found them false. You have persevered and have endured hardships for My name, and have not grown weary." (Revelation 2:2-3).

But the Ephesians had forgotten that "only one thing is {truly} needed." (Luke 10:42). Though they worked hard at doing the right things, Jesus saw directly into the condition of their heart.

Revelation 2:4

"Yet I hold this against you: You have forsaken your first love."

Most new Christians know what it means to truly love. Once we recognize the ugliness of our sin - and how Jesus died to make us clean - our heart is filled with thankfulness...and love. But often, in an attempt to "mature," we shift our focus to the "doing" of outward activities and forget how to simply love. We study more, attend more, and serve more (which are all good) - but we forget how to just sit at His feet and love.

As we mature in Christ, we must never outgrow our first love. As Jesus told the Ephesians: "Repent and do the things you did at first," (Revelation 2:5), we too must return. There will be always many opportunities to express our faith in good works - many opportunities to serve. But as we work hard, resist sin, and possibly endure great hardship, let's remember that in the end, Jesus will look directly into our heart - and we will be known by our love.

DO WHAT IT SAYS

As we continue to study God's Word, we must be reminded to never stop with just the simple accumulation of knowledge. Knowledge by itself will deceive us into a false sense of Spirituality - we must never equate an increase of knowledge with an increased closeness to God. Knowing ABOUT something is not the same as true knowledge: "The man who thinks he knows something does not yet know as he ought to know." (1 Corinthians 8:2).

It's good and wise to learn more about the Creator of the Universe as recorded in His Word. The Bible makes much more sense if we understand the context and time lines of various writings (both the Old and New Testaments). However...these facts will never accomplish their intended purpose - the purpose of drawing us closer to our Heavenly Father - until we actually do what the Word says.

James 1:22-25

"Do not merely listen to the Word, and so deceive yourselves. Do what it says. Anyone who listens to the Word but does not do what it says is like a man who looks at his face in the mirror and, after looking at himself, goes away and immediately forgets what he looks like. But the man who looks intently into the perfect law that gives freedom, and continues to do this, not forgetting what he has heard, but doing it - he will be blessed in what he does."

We will never know the true meaning of faith until we put it into practice. We cannot possibly know the peace of trusting God to work for the good in all things (Romans 8:28) until we turn our life over to Him and allow Him to work. Without putting His words into action, we become as the godless who are "always learning but never able to acknowledge the truth." (2 Timothy 3:7).

Each of us has a specific message which God desires us to receive - a truth He wants us to understand. The words of the message may be delivered through something we hear or something we read - but the words will never change our life and draw us nearer to God until we put them into practice.

God is calling us today - He is calling us to know Him and to walk with Him. The study of His Word should never cease, but we MUST take the next step. We must study with the great expectation of hearing His direction for our life. Then as we hear His Word, we must do what it says.

REQUEST A PROSPEROUS LIFE

In the middle of a very long list of genealogies, there are a few short verses about a man named Jabez who was a descendant of Judah. We never read about him again, but it appears Jabez was included because of his bold request to God...and God's response.

1 Chronicles 4:10

"Jabez cried out to the God of Israel, 'Oh, that You would bless me and enlarge my territory! Let Your hand be with me, and keep me from harm so that I will be free from pain.' And God granted his request."

Sometimes passages on asking and receiving can be difficult to teach. "How much more will your Father in heaven give good gifts to those who ask Him!" (Matthew 7:11). These passages are full of truth, but those who preach the popular prosperity gospel have abused them to say God wants everyone to be financially rich and all we must do is ask - if we can name it, we can claim it. This is far from the truth.

But, God DOES want us to prosper: "'For I know the plans I have for you,' declares the Lord, 'plans to prosper you and not to harm you, plans to give you hope and a future.'" (Jeremiah 29:11). And, He DOES want us to ask: "You do not have, because you do not ask God. When you ask, you do not receive, because you ask with wrong motives." (James 4:2-3). God has a plan to prosper us, but it is possible we do not prosper simply because we do not ask with the correct motive.

We must first understand God's definition of prosperity. A Godly prosperity has little to do with finances or possessions - and a great deal to do with peace and contentment. A prosperous life is also one which bears much fruit - one that completes the work God has assigned.

A prosperous life begins by drawing near (and remaining near) to the presence of God. Without first abiding in His presence, we won't even know what to ask for - we won't know what will allow us to "prosper." "Delight yourself in the Lord and He will give you the desire of your heart." (Psalm 37:4). As we draw near to God, He places the desires on our heart which will lead us to true prosperity - then we must ask. It is in the asking and in the expectation of the answer that we exercise our faith and prove it to be real.

Let's ask God to increase our territory - to increase our realm of influence in His Kingdom. Let's ask Him to protect us from harm and to accomplish great things in and through our life. Let's draw near to God and boldly request a prosperous life.

HE'S GOD AND WE'RE NOT

In the book of Job, we read of a man who came under severe attack by Satan. Within a short time, Job went from a man of wealth, health, and large family, to a man who was destitute, near death, and childless.

In the early stage of his trials, Job demonstrated a deep commitment God's sovereignty. After he lost his children and all his possessions, Job responded with: "Naked I came from my mother's womb, and naked I will depart. The Lord gave and the Lord has taken away; may the name of the Lord be praised." (Job 1:20-21). Then when he lost his health and his wife told him to curse God and die, Job responded with: "Shall we accept good from God, and not trouble?" (Job 2:10).

Job had a deep understanding of the verse we often quote when facing times of trial: "And we know that in all things God works for the good of those who love Him." (Romans 8:28). Despite the repeated counsel of his so-called friends, Job knew his suffering was not a punishment for sin - but at the same time, he couldn't understand why God was allowing these things to happen. He began to feel alone and abandoned.

Job 23:3-5

"If only I knew where to find Him; if only I could go to His dwelling! I would state my case before Him and fill my mouth with arguments. I would find out what He would answer me, and consider what He would say."

Our trials often cause us similar concerns. We find ourself asking where God has gone and why He is allowing such hardship. Even though we may believe God is "working all things for our good," we often search in vain to find the good in our situation. Job had these same questions. Finally, God gave His answer.

Job 38:4-5

"Where were you when I laid the earth's foundation? Tell me, if you understand. Who marked off its dimensions? Surely you know! Who stretched a measuring line across it?"

God's response continues for almost four chapters: "Can you bring forth the constellations in their season." (Job 38:32). It's as if God is reminding Job: "I'm God and you're not - you must trust Me." Many of our questions must be answered in this same manner. When we're in the middle of a trial, we must continue to believe His Word is true - even though we may not understand. We must trust in His promises, and we must remind ourselves: He's God and we're not.

CORDS OF ENCOURAGEMENT

God's Word is timeless. Solomon wrote the book of Ecclesiastes approximately 2900 years ago. In the following passage he speaks of the importance of having encouraging relationships - of the need for us to encourage others and the need to have someone in our life who will encourage us when we're down.

Ecclesiastes 4:9-12
"Two are better than one, because they have a good return for their work: If one falls down, his friend can help him up. But pity the man who falls and has no one to help him up! Also, if two lie down together, they will keep warm. But how can one keep warm alone? Though one may be overpowered, two can defend themselves. A cord of three strands is not quickly broken."

As we look out upon the body of believers scattered around the world, we notice the many ways we are different - and the many ways we are the same. We have different colors of skin, different styles of clothes, and different accents in our speech - but each of us face similar trials and temptations...and we all have the same need for encouragement.

God has taken a very diverse group of people and formed us into the Body of Christ: "Though all its parts are many, they form one body." (1 Corinthians 12:12). We put this concept to practical use as we look on other believers and understand that we desperately need each other: "If one part suffers, every part suffers with it." (1 Corinthians 12:26). When we see a Brother or Sister who is down, we must reach out to encourage them back up.

It's not always easy to recognize the best way to encourage - it sometimes takes great discernment and effort. "And let us consider how we may spur one another on toward love and good deeds." (Hebrews 10:24). Remember, the Body functions best only when each of the members are at their full potential and being guided by Christ who is the Head. This also means WE cannot be at our best until others in the Body are encouraged.

Let's take a new look at the Body of Christ today. Let's look for those who need encouragement as well as for those who will encourage us. Let's identify the strands in our life and then spend time weaving them together. Let's strengthen the Body by building unbreakable cords of encouragement.

LIONS AND BEARS

In chapter 17 of 1 Samuel, we read of David and the Philistine "Giant" named Goliath. Goliath was much larger than other people of his day: "He was over nine feet tall." (1 Samuel 17:4). For forty days he tormented the Israelites by challenging them to a battle - but no one would accept his challenge.

David was not a soldier, but his father sent him to the Israelite camp to deliver bread to his older brothers. When David heard the challenge by Goliath, he told King Saul: "Your servant will go and fight him." (1 Samuel 17:32).

Even though David had never been in battle, he had witnessed the power of God in his life. As a young shepherd, David defended the flock when a lion and a bear had come to carry away his sheep. David rescued the sheep and killed the lion and the bear. This gave him the necessary confidence to go into battle against Goliath.

1 Samuel 17:36-37
"Your servant has killed both the lion and the bear - this uncircumcised Philistine will be like one of them, because he has defied the armies of the living God. The Lord who delivered me from the paw of the lion and the paw of the bear will deliver me from the hand of this Philistine."

As we find ourselves battling our own Goliaths, we must also remember how God has defended us in the past. Our "Giant" circumstances may seem impossible to resolve - but the God who stood at our side in past battles is the same God who stands with us today.

God wants to draw us near - He wants to walk with us through each and every battle. This means we must trust He's working all things together for good - even when we can't see the good or understand His timing. Let's be encouraged by God's victories in our past - and let's look for opportunities to share these victories as an encouragement to others. As each of us face our Goliaths today, let's remember the past victories over the lions and bears.

LOVING COMMUNICATION

As we walk down the path God lays before us, we soon discover there are many forks in the road - many decision points where we must choose between God's path and the path of the world. At these critical moments, we must be able to recognize the guiding of our Heavenly Father as given through His Spirit. If we have not spent sufficient time communicating with God in prayer, we can not expect to understand His guidance in our time of greatest need.

Communication is essential to building and maintaining any relationship. A marriage which lacks communication will slowly begin to drift apart. It's not uncommon for married couples to live together for the majority of their lives and yet feel like strangers because they have failed to spend the time required to really know and understand one another.

Our relationship with God is much the same. When we accept the gift of Salvation as offered through faith in Jesus, we begin a life long relationship of love - a relationship which must be nurtured and bathed in prayer.

Psalm 5:1-3

"Give ear to my words, O Lord, consider my sighing. Listen to my cry for help, my King and my God, for to You I pray. In the morning, O Lord, You hear my voice; in the morning I lay my requests before You and wait in expectation."

David states that the morning is his dedicated time for prayer - his time to be alone with God; to share his heart and expectantly await God's direction. But God has not specified a preferred time for prayer. In fact, Paul encourages us to maintain a constant state of communion with God when he says to "pray continuously." (1 Thessalonians 5:17). Any time is the right time for prayer - but we should strive for consistency.

For our prayers to have meaning, they must originate from a sincere heart. They must be motivated by a desire to strengthen the relationship, to increase our understanding - to deepen our love. We must value our time with God above all else: "One thing I ask of the Lord, this is what I seek: that I may dwell in the house of the Lord all the days of my life." (Psalm 27:4).

Let's make sure our love doesn't fade. Let's set aside time each day to be alone with God - time that will ensure we can hear His voice. Let's strengthen our relationship with God through regular and loving communication.

FILLED WITH AWE

The first believers of the risen Christ were gathered together in Jerusalem. They were led by the apostles who had walked and talked with Jesus. They knew the power of the Holy Spirit and "spoke the Word of God boldly." (Acts 4:31). They fellowshipped together with great intimacy (Acts 2:44-47) - but most important...

Acts 2:43

> *"Everyone was filled with awe, and many wonders and miraculous signs were done by the apostles."*

Being "filled with awe" means to have an overwhelming sense of "reverent fear - wonder and amazement." This is the same meaning used by Solomon when he wrote: "The fear of the Lord is the beginning of wisdom." (Proverbs 9:10). Our understanding of God begins with a reverent fear which brings us to our knees in worship.

Have we become complacent with the wonders of God? Have we forgotten the miracle of: "In the beginning God created the heavens and the earth." (Genesis 1:1). Or the marvel of: "So God created man in His own image... male and female He created them." (Genesis 1:27). Or the awesome wonder of His love: "But God demonstrates His own love for us in this: While we were still sinners, Christ died for us." (Romans 5:8).

These verses alone should inspire a lifetime of praise - but God has given us much more. Through the Apostle John, we have something the early believers didn't have - we have a picture of God's throne room in Heaven.

Revelation 4:2-8

> *"And there before me was a throne in heaven with someone sitting on it... A rainbow, resembling an emerald, encircled the throne.... Around the throne, were four living creatures.... Day and night they never stop saying: 'Holy, holy, holy is the Lord God Almighty, who was, and is, and is to come.'"*

Let's reflect on the miracles of God's creation, His plan of redemption through Jesus, and the true majesty of His Kingdom. Many amazing things will occur in our personal life and in the life of our local church if we return to the complete reverence and wonder of our Lord - if our lives are once again filled with awe.

CONSIDER HIM WHO ENDURED

As we walk together on this wonderful journey, we must assume a certain level of responsibility for one another. We must lift up our Brothers and Sisters when they are down and we must remind one another that God is near - that our trials will soon fade: "Encourage one another daily, as long as it is called Today!" (Hebrews 3:13). But we also have a responsibility to encourage without enabling a complaining or selfish attitude.

We began this journey through faith in Jesus. We believed: "For God so loved the world that He gave His one and only Son, that whoever believes in Him shall not perish but have eternal life." (John 3:16). We believed that Jesus died on a cross for the forgiveness of our sins so we could live with Him for all eternity.

Jesus endured ridicule and humiliation from His accusers, and overwhelming pain on the cross because He loved us dearly. The joy of seeing our restored relationship with the Father allowed Him to endure. His sacrifice brought us Salvation - His endurance should bring us perseverance and strength.

Hebrews 12:3

"Consider Him who endured such opposition from sinful men, so that you will not grow weary and lose heart."

There are going to be days when the burden seems extra heavy - days when the attacks come fast and furious. When we begin to feel weary, we usually seek someone who will agree with us and confirm the difficulty of our life.

This can be comforting for a short period - but we must not dwell in this condition. We must pick up our load, hold our head high, and continue down the path with our eyes fixed on Jesus. We will not lose heart if we focus on His love. We will not grow weary if we consider Him who endured.

INTO HIS HANDS

A life which is lived by fully trusting God begins with simple faith and grows as we apply that faith in a variety of circumstances. Not many of us begin with the faith of Peter: "Lord, if it's You, tell me to come to You on the water." (Matthew 14:28). Rather, we begin with small doses of trust and grow as we actually see the promises of God hold true.

Prior to crossing into the promised land, Moses told the people of Israel: "Do not be afraid, for the Lord goes with you; He will never leave you nor forsake you." (Deuteronomy 31:6). This is one of the many promises we have from God today. The writer of Hebrews encourages us to apply this promise (in faith) in order to live a life of contentment: "Keep your lives free from the love of money and be content with what you have because God has said: 'Never will I leave you; never will I forsake you.'" (Hebrews 13:5).

But living a life of true contentment can be difficult. Everyday we are bombarded with things which attempt to steal our joy. We must continually believe the truth of God's Word and allow our faith to mature. This maturity is developed every time we take a step of faith - even if our steps seem very small. With each step, we more clearly see the truth of God's promises...until finally, we take the step into total commitment.

Psalm 31:5

"Into Your hands I commit my spirit; redeem me, O Lord, the God of truth."

At some point in our Christian walk, we must make a decision. We are either going to live by faith or we are going to live by fear. We either fully commit our life to God or we continue to fight life's battles with our own limited strength and continue to be swayed by our own deceptive desires.

One day, we will no longer tip toe at the edge of the water - we will truly believe the water will hold. Let's make that day be today! Let's stand before our Heavenly Father and trust Him with all our heart. Let's step out in faith and fully commit our body, soul, and spirit into His hands.

HIGHLY VALUED MIST

Many people today struggle with insecurities, low self esteem, and general feelings of inadequacy. While it's true that we should "in humility consider others better than ourselves," (Philippians 2:3), we also must have a sense of identity, purpose, and worth. And while it's also true that in the context of eternity, we are "a mist that appears for a little while and then vanishes," (James 4:14), this "mist" is dearly loved by the Creator of the Universe.

Our worth does not come from the things of this world which all pass away, it comes from our Heavenly Father who has adopted us as heirs into His Kingdom!

Romans 8:15-17

"You received the Spirit of sonship. And by Him we cry, 'Abba, Father.' The Spirit Himself testifies with our spirit that we are God's children. Now if we are children, then we are heirs - heirs of God and co-heirs with Christ."

The inheritance we receive through this adoption makes everything of the world seem extremely insignificant. Our Heavenly inheritance is infinitely superior in quality and will last for all eternity - we are "co-heirs with Christ!"

As this world tries to pull us down, remember our Father owns "the cattle on a thousand hills" (Psalm 50:10) - in fact, He created the cattle AND the hills. As others try to continually show us our faults, remember that one day we will be made perfect and walk down streets of "pure gold, like transparent glass." (Revelation 21:21).

Let's pull these truths into a victorious Christian life. Let's hold on very loosely to anything of the world which artificially determines our worth and passionately cling to our worth in Christ. "For what is seen is temporary, but what is unseen is eternal." (2 Corinthians 4:18). Let's live our life as a "vanishing mist" while remembering we are co-heirs with Jesus in the Kingdom of God - let's live our life as a highly valued mist.

GIVE FROM THE HEART

In the book of Malachi, God calls the people back to the laws He established 800 years earlier with Moses. God spoke of the necessity of a pure sacrifice (Malachi 1:7-8), and the need for the priests to speak the truth (Malachi 2:7-8). Through Malachi, God also addressed the issue of the tithe.

Malachi 3:8-10

"Will a man rob God? Yet you rob Me. But you ask, 'How do we rob You?' In tithes and offerings. You are under a curse - the whole nation of you - because you are robbing Me. Bring the whole tithe into the storehouse, that there may be food in My house."

The principle of an offering to God began with Cain and Able (Genesis 4:3-4). Many generations later, Abraham demonstrated the concept of the tithe when he gave the priest, Melchizedek, "a tenth of everything." (Genesis 14:20). But a systematic process of tithing was not established until several hundred years later with the law of Moses. (Leviticus 27:30-33).

Jesus came as the complete fulfillment of the law (Matthew 5:15). Through faith in Jesus, we have been freed from the bondage of the law: "You are not under the law, but under grace." (Romans 6:14). This does not mean we have the freedom to abuse the law (Romans 6:15) - it means we are now to live with the intent of the law inscribed on our heart.

The law says "Thou shalt not kill," but Jesus says to live by the intent of the law and not even have hatred in our heart toward our brother. (Matthew 5:21-22). The law also says "Thou shalt not commit adultery," but Jesus says to even keep lust out of our heart (Matthew 5:27-28).

The intent of all the law is that God is to be the Lord over ALL areas of our life. When we debate about how much to give and where to give, we miss the real issue - He is Lord! As we draw closer to our Heavenly Father - as we release our self-ownership and allow Him to be Lord - we will give. We will give of our time; we will give of our talents....and, we will give of our finances. When He is Lord, we will not give according to a "formula" of the law - we will give according to the law's intent - we will give joyfully and we will give from the heart.

DID GOD REALLY SAY

The first two chapters of the Bible tell how God "created the heavens and the earth." (Genesis 1:1). God placed Adam in the Garden of Eden and created Eve to be his companion and helper. Life was good in the garden - but it didn't take long for the deception of the devil to really mess things up.

God had given Adam and Eve the freedom to eat from any tree in the garden - any tree except one: "You must not eat from the tree of the knowledge of good and evil, for when you eat of it you will surely die." (Genesis 2:17). When the devil first confronted Eve, he began by causing her to doubt what God had said.

Genesis 3:1

"He said to the woman, 'Did God really say, You must not eat from any tree in the garden?'"

Eve knew what God had said - but her lack of conviction resulted in her believing the devil's lie: "You will not surely die. For God knows that when you eat of it your eyes will be opened, and you will be like God." (Genesis 3:4-5). But the truth was that God really said: "When you eat of it you will surely die." - and He meant it!

In the several thousand years since that first confrontation, the tactics of the devil are still pretty much the same. His first attack is always to get us to doubt the Word of God.

Did God really say: "Whoever believes in Him shall not perish but have eternal life." (John 3:16)?

Did God really say: "Do not worry about your life, what you will eat or drink; or about your body, what you will wear. But seek first His kingdom and His righteousness, and all these things will be given to you as well." (Matthew 6:25,33)?

Did God really say: "Love the Lord your God with all your heart and with all your soul and with all your mind and with all your strength." (Mark 12:30)?

If we are not firm in our conviction that God's Word is true, we too will become vulnerable to the devil's attacks of doubt and will soon begin to believe his twisted lies. Let's prepare ourselves by studying God's Word and praying for wisdom to know His truth. Let's be ready to give a bold and unshakable answer whenever our faith is tested with the question...Did God really say?

BOUNDARY LINE OF TRUTH

In the message, "Did God Really Say," we saw how the devil began his deception with Eve by causing her to doubt what God said: "Did God really say, 'You must not eat...'?" (Genesis 3:1). He then said God had lied and was actually keeping her from something beneficial: "God knows that when you eat of it your eyes will be opened, and you will be like God, knowing good and evil." (Genesis 3:5).

The devil convinced Eve that disobeying God (in just this one instance) would be the right thing to do. After all, she would become more like God and that must be the proper path to follow.

Genesis 3:6

"When the woman saw that the fruit of the tree was good for food and pleasing to the eye, and also desirable for gaining wisdom, she took some and ate it."

Eve had seen the fruit before - she already knew it looked good - but God had established a boundary line which until now she had not crossed. But when the devil presented his twisted version of the truth, this line began to shift. Eve became unsure about absolute right and wrong and saw the line as something she could control - she changed the definition of right in order to violate God's command.

God has shown each of us the boundary line between right and wrong - we know the truth. God's line is not subject to our control and we are not given the freedom to cross the line depending on the circumstances or perceived benefit.

Many of us become deceived by simple justifications: "I know this is wrong, but it's important for me to gain the experience - my increased wisdom will eventually help others." Or: "I know this is wrong, but this 'little' sin may actually keep me from a bigger sin down the road - God certainly doesn't want me to be consumed with temptation." Or: "I know this is wrong, but it will eventually bring glory to God."

It's God's desire that we follow His path each and every day - without ANY shortcuts. He will NEVER direct us to sin in order to accomplish His perfect will for our life. If a path contains sin, we can be sure it's NOT God's path. Let's trust Him to absolutely direct our every step. Let's draw so close to our Heavenly Father that all deception is exposed. Let's walk without compromise and not cross His boundary line of truth.

WHERE ARE YOU

The devil deceived Eve and caused her to disobey God's command. The deception began by first causing Eve to doubt what God said and continued by saying God had not been truthful.

Eve justified her disobedience as being in her best interest, ate the fruit from the forbidden tree, and gave some to her willing husband. As soon as they ate the fruit, they became aware that they were naked and covered themselves with leaves.

Genesis 3:8-9
"Then the man and his wife heard the sound of the Lord God as He was walking in the garden in the cool of the day, and they hid from the Lord God among the trees of the garden. But the Lord God called to the man, 'Where are you?'"

"Where are you?" is an interesting choice of words for the all-knowing Creator of the Universe. God knew exactly where Adam was hiding. He wasn't searching through the bushes trying to find His lost creation: "Aaaaaadaaaaammm....Where aarrrrrree yoouuuuuuu?" No, God was speaking directly to Adam: "Adam, why are you here? Why are you in this condition? Do you know where you are?"

Adam's willful disobedience caused him to tremble as he answered: "I was afraid because I was naked; so I hid." (Genesis 3:10). Adam was lost. Somehow, even in the paradise of the garden, Adam and Eve had wandered in their relationship with God. They were alone when the deceptions of the devil took hold - and now their sin caused them to hide from God.

ALL sin has its beginning in a separation from God - in a wandering from His presence. We cannot sin if we remain in His presence. As we truly live our life "in Christ," the conviction of the Spirit is so great that we are not able to walk down the path of temptation that leads to sin.

Do we know where we are? The Apostle Paul tells us to "Examine yourselves," (2 Corinthians 13:5). A life outside of God's presence will begin to believe the lie and become susceptible to temptation. A life immersed in sin will desire to run and hide.

Let's return to a life of worship where Jesus is the focus of everything we do and say. Let's honestly examine our life and evaluate our closeness with God. Let's make sure we're abiding in His presence when God asks...Where are you?

SHINY STONES

There are many types of monkeys that can be captured with nothing more than a hollow wooden ball and a few shiny stones. The wooden ball contains a hole just large enough for the opened hand of the monkey to pass through. The shiny stones are placed inside the ball and the ball is then tied to a tree.

The curious monkey reaches into the hollow ball and grasps the stones, but then finds his hand will no longer pass through the hole while it is clinging to the stones. The monkey fights to free his hand but will not drop the stones and is therefore easily captured.

This is a fun story - but it really isn't true. Monkeys are actually much smarter than this illustration makes them appear. But I wonder if we can say the same for ourselves.

Jesus had chosen His twelve disciples and was giving them instructions before they were sent out to minister. He told them where to go and some of the hardships to expect. He also told them one of the great secrets of a successful journey.

Matthew 10:39

"Whoever finds his life will lose it, and whoever loses his life for My sake will find it."

The New Living Translation gives a nice rendering of this same verse: "If you cling to your life, you will lose it; but if you give it up for Me, you will find it."

We are absolutely saved by grace through faith in Jesus Christ (Ephesians 2:8) - but this faith must be so complete that it causes us to even change our way of thinking. No longer can we cling to the pleasures and values of the world; we must let go and present ourselves to God as a living sacrifice (Romans 12:1).

Life without complete surrender is empty. We may think we're on the road to happiness, but if we look close we'll see a handful of stones and an enemy who is ready to pounce. If we want to find true life, we must have a faith in which we lose ourselves to the will of our Heavenly Father - we must let go of our shiny stones.

PRAYING FOR CORN HUSKS

In the parable of the prodigal son, we see a rebellious young man demanding what he felt was rightfully his: "Father, give me my share of the estate." (Luke 15:12). This disrespectful attitude grew until the son no longer wanted to live under his father's roof. He set off to find his "own way" and proceeded to spend his entire inheritance.

The son took a job feeding pigs and hit bottom when he longed to eat the husks being given to the pigs. God used these very harsh circumstances to bring the prodigal son to repentance.

Luke 15:17-18
"When he came to his senses, he said, 'How many of my father's hired men have food to spare, and here I am starving to death! I will set out and go back to my father and say to him: Father, I have sinned against heaven and against you.'"

Before the son left home, I'm sure the father tried to give him some wise counsel - but apparently, the son had lessons to learn which only corn husks could teach.

God reminds us of one of His basic truths: There is absolutely NOTHING more important in life than being brought to Salvation through faith in Jesus Christ.

Those of us with prodigals must continue to pray and continue to speak a message of truth at every opportunity. But we must also release them to the perfect working of our Lord. Yes, we should pray for their protection - but we must also ask God to use ANY method necessary to bring them into a right relationship with Himself...even if this means we are praying for corn husks!

A LONG WAY OFF

In the message, "Praying For Corn Husks," we looked at the parable of the prodigal son and saw how God used difficult circumstances (corn husks) to lead the son to repentance and bring him home.

As we continue with the parable, we see the repentant son recognize his sin and start back home. He has prepared a speech to give his father and is now ready to completely submit: "Make me like one of your hired men." (Luke 15:19). But before the son can give his apology - before he can tell his father about the corn husks - before he can "prove" his repentance...

Luke 15:20
"But while he was still a long way off, his father saw him and was filled with compassion for him; he ran to his son, threw his arms around him and kissed him."

When the father saw his son had returned, he was overjoyed and wanted to celebrate: "Bring the fatted calf...for this son of mine was dead and is alive again; he was lost and is found." (Luke 15:23,24).

The scripture isn't clear about what turmoil occurred when the prodigal son left home. We're never told of the father's pain - but I assure you it was there. It's not clear how long the son was away - but I promise the father spent many anxious moments worrying about his son. And yet, when the son returned, there was unconditional acceptance and forgiveness.

This parable is primarily meant for the relationship between our Heavenly Father and His children. When we turn to Him in faith, He accepts us without requiring that we earn His love or demonstrate our worth. But this parable also applies to relationships with anyone who has caused us pain or concern.

When an attempt is made at restoration, we must act as a catalyst - not a hedge of thorns! We must love and forgive as Christ first loved and forgave us - not make the other person earn their way back into our life. When they begin to return, let's believe the best and be filled with compassion and joy - even while they are a long way off.

LOVE ENOUGH TO LET GO

The last two messages have considered the parable of the prodigal son (Luke 15:11-32). We saw how God used great hardship to bring a son to repentance - and we saw how the father rejoiced as the son returned home. It's significant that there is no mention of the father between the time the son left home and the time he returned.

We know the father loved his son by the way he rejoiced at his return. We also know that the father knew something of the son's condition: "This son of mine was dead and is alive again." (Luke 15:24). Reports about the son must have been sent back home - for his brother was quick to express disgust to his father: "This son of yours who has squandered your property with prostitutes comes home." (Luke 15:30). And yet, while he was away, the father never stepped in to "rescue" his prodigal son.

James 1:2-4

"Consider it pure joy, my brothers, whenever you face trials of many kinds, because you know that the testing of your faith develops perseverance. Perseverance must finish its work so that you may be mature and complete, not lacking anything."

We often reference this passage when there is need for encouragement during times of trial. These verses tell us to do more than just "hang on" during the hard times - we are to trust God so fully that we actually rejoice because we know He is using these trials to make us complete.

Many of us understand and at least try to apply these verses in our own life. But it's an additional step of faith (a big step) to apply these verses in the life of others - especially those we love.

If we are to rejoice in our own trials because of the good being worked within us, there is also a sense in which we should rejoice in the trials of others. God is not only working in our life - He's working in lives all around us.

As painful as it must have been, the father allowed God to complete His work - even though it meant his son would eat with the pigs! And yes, this father loved his son.

When someone we love goes astray, let's continue to lift them up in prayer. Let's always let them know they are loved - and listen very carefully for God to direct when and if we are to act. Let's allow Him to finish the work He's begun - let's love enough to let go.

THE OTHER SON

This is the final message in a series on the prodigal son. We've looked at the prodigal son and how God used hardship to bring him back home - and we've considered the role of the father; both in terms of letting the prodigal go and in terms of accepting him back. But the one person who is often overlooked is the son who remained at home.

He was the son who quietly watched his younger brother make disrespectful demands: "Give me my share of the estate." (Luke 15:12). He was the son who stayed at home to work the fields while his brother "squandered his wealth in wild living." (Luke 15:13). And he was the son who refused to celebrate his brother's return. He became angry that his father had so eagerly welcomed his wayward brother back home: "All these years I've been slaving for you and never disobeyed your orders. Yet you never gave me even a young goat." (Luke 15:29).

This was the son who walked the straight and narrow - but he missed his opportunity to receive true blessings as he walked.

Luke 15:31
"'My son,' the father said, 'you are always with me, and every-thing I have is yours.'"

The son had been "slaving" in the hope of some kind of future blessing - but he missed the real blessing of walking day after day with his father and having free access to everything his father owned.

As believers in the saving grace of Jesus Christ, we understand that people can be saved at any point in their life - regardless of past sins. The thief on the cross received his Salvation only moments before he died. But there is always part of us that cries "foul!" Somehow it doesn't seem fair.

This attitude shows we also have missed the blessing of walking with our Lord. Eternity in Heaven is not a reward for right living - it is a gift to those who believe. Obedience is not to be a burden. We should never feel we're "slaving" under His commands. Rather, we are to joyfully follow because we know that only in Him is there true peace, true contentment...true blessings!

Let's follow our Lord with a firm perspective of eternity - but let's never become so focused on the future that we miss the blessings given to us today. Let's enjoy every day with our Heavenly Father and rejoice every time a repentant heart falls into His arms. Let's not make the sad mistake of the other son.

GO TO NINEVEH

The subject of God's will is often one of great concern to the growing Christian. Those who have accepted the forgiving grace of Jesus now have a desire to live a life which brings Him glory and honor. We have read about presenting ourself as a living sacrifice (Romans 12:1), and we're ready to do His will - but what exactly does God want us to do...where does He want us to go?

Fortunately, much of God's will is found directly in His Word and is meant for all of us. It's God's will that we live a life which is pure and holy (1 Thessalonians 4:3-7), and obey His commands (John 15:10). It's God's will that we love Him with all our heart, soul, mind, and strength (Mark 12:30), that we remain in Him and bear fruit (John 15:1-8), that we forgive others (Matthew 6:14-15), love others (1 John 4:7), and share the message of Jesus with others (Matthew 28:19-20). It's also God's will that we always rejoice, continuously pray, and give thanks in all circumstances (1 Thessalonians 5:16-18).

Take another look at this list. We refer to this as God's "general" will - and there's enough here to occupy us for a lifetime. There's no need to frantically search for God's specific will for our life - when He's ready, He will certainly call...then we must be prepared to follow.

Jonah was a man who had the "opportunity" to clearly hear God's specific will.

Jonah 1:2
> *"Go to the great city of Nineveh and preach against it, because its wickedness has come up before Me."*

When God reveals His specific will for our life, it is done clearly and with a definite purpose. We then must choose whether to obey. Jonah tried to run from God and spent three days inside a giant fish. After the fish vomited Jonah onto dry land, God calmly revealed His will a second time: "Go to the great city of Nineveh and proclaim to it the message I give you." (Jonah 3:2). This time Jonah obeyed.

There are parts of God's will which are already revealed - we should do these things now! For the part of God's will which is specific to our life, we must listen intently, pray diligently, and wait very patiently - but when His direction arrives, let's not run away...let's eagerly go to Nineveh!

A SECURE SERVANT

The night before Jesus was crucified, He was celebrating the Passover with His disciples. We traditionally call this the Last Supper. Jesus knew this would be the last time He would eat with His disciples - He knew in just one more day He would be hung on a cross to die.

Knowing He only had a few short hours remaining with this select group, Jesus wanted to use His time wisely. He would never again have such direct contact, so He wanted to leave a lasting impression of what it meant to truly follow Him.

John 13:3-5

"Jesus knew that the Father had put all things under His power, and that He had come from God and was returning to God; so He got up from the meal, took off His outer clothing, and wrapped a towel around His waist. After that, He poured water into a basin and began to wash His disciples' feet, drying them with the towel that was wrapped around Him."

Without using words, Jesus may have given His greatest sermon. At this moment, Jesus was absolutely secure in who He was and where He was going: "He had come from God and was returning to God." But He was not proud or arrogant in His security - instead, His security allowed Him to be completely humble and to serve His disciples by washing their feet.

Our Heavenly Father desires for us to have this same level of security in Him. He wants us to KNOW we are His children and where we will spend eternity. He wants us to have a security which allows us to serve Him with joy and know that nothing "will be able to separate us from the love of God that is in Christ Jesus our Lord." (Romans 8:39).

With only one day to live, Jesus continued to teach. At this last meal, He demonstrated how we are to be transformed into a secure servant.

SUNDAY'S COMING

In one sense, the Friday before Easter represents one of the darkest days of our history - this is the day we remember the crucifixion of Jesus Christ. The previous night, in a place called Gethsemane, Jesus was betrayed by one of His closest followers and abandoned by all the rest. In the morning, when the Roman governor (Pilate) asked the crowd what he should do with Jesus, they said with one voice; "Crucify Him!" (Matthew 27:22).

Remember - this was the Creator of the Universe: "Who, being in very nature God...made Himself nothing, taking the very nature of a servant, being made in human likeness." (Philippians 2:6-7). Jesus became a man for one purpose - to pay the penalty for our sin and bring us into an everlasting relationship with our Heavenly Father.

The Creator of the Universe, who had all the power of Heaven within His command, allowed Himself to be whipped, crowned with thorns, and spit upon. He allowed Himself to be nailed to a cross and hung until all life left His body.

We know that although Friday remembers a day that was dark and bleak, the glory of Sunday was coming. "He must be killed and on the third day be raised to life." (Luke 9:22). On the third day The Sacrificial Lamb was to rise and return to His rightful place: "He sat down at the right hand of God." (Hebrews 10:12).

On the morning of the third day, some women came to look at the tomb where Jesus had been buried.

Matthew 28:5-6
"The angel said to the women, 'Do not be afraid, for I know that you are looking for Jesus, who was crucified. He is not here; He is risen, just as He said. Come and see the place where He lay.'"

There continues to be debate regarding the actual days of His crucifixion. But let's not lose site that there was a day when the greatest gift of love was given. Let's remember the cost of the cross and the incredible sacrifice He offered for us all. Let's also look forward to the day He rose and sat on the throne - the day He was victorious over death. On this Friday before Easter, let's prepare our hearts with great anticipation...Sunday's coming!

SUNDAY HAS COME

In the message, "Sunday's Coming," we were encouraged to look forward to the glory of Sunday and the resurrection of Jesus. Friday was a day for us to remember when Jesus was whipped and nailed to the cross. Yet, through those thoughts of unimaginable pain and suffering, we knew victory was in sight - we knew Sunday was coming!

But now we must examine our life and ask: Has Sunday really come?

Easter Sunday is the day we remember the empty tomb and our risen Lord. On this morning, Mary Magdalene and her friends saw the empty tomb first hand and immediately ran to tell the disciples: "But they did not believe the women, because their words seemed to them like nonsense." (Luke 24:11). Even after Peter saw the empty tomb for himself, he was perplexed: "He went away, wondering to himself what had happened." (Luke 24:12).

The disciples had walked with Jesus and listened to Him teach about this day - but they still did not understand. It wasn't until Jesus appeared to the disciples later that same evening that the events began to make sense: "Then He opened their minds so they could understand the Scriptures." (Luke 24:45).

In an instant, everything fit into place. They finally understood how all the Old Testament Scripture pointed to the coming of Jesus and how He would be the sacrifice for the forgiveness of our sins. They saw the predictions of His death and of His resurrection. They finally saw Him as much more than a good teacher, much more than even a mighty King - He was the Savior, the Son of God!

Romans 1:4
"And who through the Spirit of holiness was declared with power to be the Son of God by His resurrection from the dead: Jesus Christ our Lord."

The resurrection was God's declaration to the world: This is My Son! The resurrection lets us know that "with God ALL things are possible." (Matthew 19:26). The resurrection gives us the assurance that every one of His promises will come to pass. If Christ is truly risen, then how can the trials of this world possibly lead to defeat?

Let's place our faith in Jesus at the cross for the forgiveness of our sins and live in the promise and power of His resurrection. Let's live with the true understanding that He has risen...Sunday has come!

HIS BURDEN IS LIGHT

Each of us have been called into ministry. We are given the charge to tell others of the way to the Father through faith in Jesus. Paul calls this the ministry of reconciliation: "We are therefore Christ's ambassadors, as though God were making his appeal through us." (2 Corinthians 5:20).

Our specific roles in this ministry may differ, but we must all be involved - we are all needed. But ministry (in any form) can be hard. There is more work to be done in the field than we can possibly accomplish - our "job" is never complete. This has the potential for great stress if we don't maintain a sense of our true purpose and a sense of Who's really in charge.

Matthew 11:28-30
"Come to Me, all you who are weary and burdened, and I will give you rest. Take My yoke upon you and learn from Me, for I am gentle and humble in heart, and you will find rest for your souls. For My yoke is easy and My burden is light."

A yoke is a dual harness used by oxen to plow the fields. Jesus says to take up His yoke and join Him in working the field. He's already pulling the load and wants us to attach ourselves to the other harness. As we do, we will discover a well-defined row in bad need of plowing - we will also find a load which is easy to bear.

But plowing can become tedious. We begin to increase the pace. We look for ways to accomplish more and begin to see the many weeds scattered in other rows and other fields. We begin to wander and our load becomes increasingly heavy - we soon find we have unhitched from His yoke.

More is not always better and faster is not always the desired result. It's interesting that Jesus says our main task as we take up His yoke is to "learn from Him." It's as if walking by His side is really enough. The field will still get plowed, but in the process we will be blessed with a closer and deeper relationship.

If our burden has become heavy, let's determine if we are properly "hitched" to His yoke and aligned to His row. A heavy burden requires some adjustments - maybe an adjustment in attitude; maybe an adjustment in priority. Let's ask our Heavenly Father for guidance and where to find rest for our soul. Let's take up His yoke and remember - His burden is light!

LIGHT AND MOMENTARY

There is no more dramatic example of a Christ-changed life than the Apostle Paul. While on his way to the city of Damascus to capture Christians and put them in jail, Jesus blinded Paul with a flash of light and asked: "Why do you persecute Me?" (Acts 9:4). When Paul asked who was speaking, Jesus replied: "I am Jesus, whom you are persecuting. Now get up and go into the city, and you will be told what you must do." (Acts 9:5-6).

We're not sure why God chose Paul - but He did. Jesus clearly identifies Paul as "My chosen instrument to carry My name before the Gentiles and their kings and before the people of Israel." (Acts 9:15). This special selection did not make Paul a perfect man, but he certainly was gifted with a close relationship with Jesus Christ as well as special insight into scripture.

Paul suffered many hardships and trials during his life, but God had taught him "the secret of being content in any and every situation, whether well fed or hungry, whether living in plenty or in want." (Philippians 4:12). Paul had a clear understanding of his eternal future with Jesus.

2 Corinthians 4:16-17
"Therefore we do not lose heart. Though outwardly we are wasting away, yet inwardly we are being renewed day by day. For our light and momentary troubles are achieving for us an eternal glory that far outweighs them all."

Paul faced terribly harsh circumstances - and yet he referred to them as "light and momentary." Paul had learned that the "secret" of a contented life is a change of focus - a change to an eternal perspective.

Rather than thinking of our life with a beginning and an end - typically lasting less than 100 years - we truly must view our life as lasting for all eternity. With this perspective, anything we face today (even if it lasts for MANY years) is only momentary - and any burden we carry (even if it seems VERY heavy) is really very light.

"I have told you these things, so that in me you may have peace. In this world you will have trouble. But take heart! I have overcome the world." (John 16:33). Let's take a good look at our life with an eternal perspective - let's be renewed and view ALL our trouble as light and momentary.

LIFT HIM UP

When Jesus told us to "go and make disciples of all nations" (Matthew 28:19), what was He really asking us to do?

Jesus said: "No one can come to Me unless the Father who sent Me draws him." (John 6:44). So what is our responsibility? After all, since only those who are drawn by God will ever come to Jesus, what is our role?

Paul reminds us of our responsibility in his letter to the Romans: "How, then, can they call on the one they have not believed in? And how can they believe in the one of whom they have not heard? And how can they hear without someone preaching to them? And how can they preach unless they are sent?" (Romans 10:14-15).

For someone to be saved, they must be presented the gospel message and they must be drawn by God. Jesus ties these together when He says:

John 12:32
"But I, when I am lifted up from the earth, will draw all men to Myself."

No matter what ministry we are involved in (whether pastoring a large church, witnessing to a friend, or just letting someone know we care), our focus must always be to lift up the name of Jesus Christ. Remember that no one is ever saved by being drawn to us or our ministry.

We are all called to minister - and the promise is if we lift up the name of Jesus, they will be drawn. Paul understood this simplicity when he said: "I resolved to know nothing while I was with you except Jesus Christ and Him crucified." (1 Corinthians 2:2).

So how do we go and make disciples of all nations? Each of us is to live a life pleasing to God, go where He sends us, help to send others, and in ALL we do - lift Him up.

TASTE AND SEE

I have a new favorite candy! The other night, my daughter and I went to the store and she grabbed a large bag of M&M's from the candy discount shelf. I'm not sure if M&M's are found all around the world, but I've enjoyed these basic candy coated chocolates for MANY years. We didn't even make it home before I had opened the bag and poured out a handful.

My mouth was watering before the candy even hit my tongue - but as soon as I bit down I knew something was different. These weren't my normal M&M's! These chocolates were light and crispy - and though I didn't think it was possible, they tasted even better. But as much as I love the taste of my new favorite candy (Crispy M&M's), I can never "prove" to you that they taste good - you will need to try them for yourself.

Sooner or later, it seems like all of us are confronted by someone who says: "Prove God is real." Maybe that person is a co-worker or a family member - or maybe to some degree it's us. We may desire to draw closer to God, but we're looking for some firmer evidence before we take that step of faith.

God can never be "proved" to someone who does not already believe. By the world's understanding, there will always be a way for unbelief to prevail. And even if absolute proof was available, this would not always lead to belief: "If they do not listen to Moses and the Prophets, they will not be convinced even if someone rises from the dead." (Luke 16:31).

Paul reminds us that "it is by grace you have been saved, through faith" (Ephesians 2:8), and we know that "faith is being sure of what we hope for and certain of what we do not see." (Hebrews 11:1). Receiving the saving gift of eternal life (as well as every subsequent step we take closer to God) will ALWAYS involve a step of faith which requires us to believe beyond the "facts."

Psalm 34:8
"Taste and see that the Lord is good; blessed is the man who takes refuge in Him."

At some point, we must simply let go, fall into His arms, and taste His goodness. I have experienced the goodness of God - and I will testify with all sincerity that absolutely nothing can compare to the joy of walking with the Lord...but I can't prove it. Each of us must experience this truth for ourself - each of us must taste and see!

A TIME OF WAITING

As Paul was returning to Jerusalem at the end of his third missionary journey, he knew he would face many difficulties: "I only know that in every city the Holy Spirit warns me that prison and hardships are facing me." (Acts 20:23). However, he also knew he must eventually visit Rome. (Acts 19:21).

In less than 10 days after arriving in Jerusalem, Paul was arrested. He probably didn't realize it at the time, but his journey to Rome had just begun.

Paul's journey would last about two and a half years and include many legal and physical trials - it would also include many opportunities to demonstrate his faith in Jesus Christ. Surprisingly, it also included a long period where Paul had nothing to do but sit in prison and wait for an occasional visit with the Governor.

Acts 24:25
"As Paul discoursed on righteousness, self-control and the judgment to come, Felix was afraid and said, 'That's enough for now! You may leave. When I find it convenient, I will send for you.'"

Paul remained in prison for two years until another governor arrived and finally transferred Paul to Rome so his case could be heard before Caesar. This must have been a very difficult time for someone accustomed to being so actively involved in ministry. Paul was treated well in this prison, but after receiving specific instructions to minister in Rome, two years must have felt like a very long time.

We're never really told of God's reason for this waiting period. Many times, waiting is necessary to allow other events to occur and other people to be properly positioned - and many times, waiting is necessary simply because we need a rest.

Paul was about to face his most challenging journey and possibly his most significant ministry opportunity. "Take courage! As you have testified about Me in Jerusalem, so you must also testify in Rome." (Acts 23:11). Paul would face a severe storm, shipwreck, snakebite, and threats on his life. He would also be given the opportunity to minister to the leaders of the Roman Empire.

Our present circumstances always serve a purpose. If we have earnestly sought God's direction and have not received specific instructions, it's very possible He is simply saying wait. Wait and be refreshed - wait and spend time in His presence...wait and prepare. Let's rejoice in the Lord ALWAYS - even while we are in a time of waiting.

CLOUD OF WITNESSES

The eleventh chapter of Hebrews is often referred to as the Great Hall of Faith. The chapter begins with a clear definition of faith: "Now faith is being sure of what we hope for and certain of what we do not see." (Hebrews 11:1). It then proceeds to describe many people from the Old Testament who were commended for their faith. The list of the faithful includes Able, Noah, Abraham, Moses, Gideon, Samson, David, and many others.

At the end of this impressive list, we read that even though they were faithful, "none of them received what had been promised." (Hebrews 11:39). Their glory or reward is being postponed until "together with us would they be made perfect." (Hebrews 11:40).

It's as if the faithful from the past are now watching us with great excitement and anticipation - knowing that one day we will meet and together receive our eternal reward. This is an awesome picture which leads us directly into chapter twelve.

Hebrews 12:1

"Therefore, since we are surrounded by such a great cloud of witnesses, let us throw off everything that hinders and the sin that so easily entangles, and let us run with perseverance the race marked out for us."

This cloud of witnesses is made up of the men and women of faith listed in chapter eleven. It now includes the New Testament believers as well as Christians throughout the last 2000 years. As we run the race and sometimes fall, the cloud of witnesses are in the stands cheering us on and encouraging our steps.

Abraham: "Just pick up your stuff and go - God will lead the way. Trust Him with everything!" (Genesis 12:1).

Moses: "I didn't think I was good enough either. Don't worry, God will provide the tools you need." (Exodus 3-4).

David: "You can conquer that giant - God is at your side!" (1 Samuel 17:37).

Paul: "Keep running! Finish the race!" (2 Timothy 4:5-7).

My Grandpa: "Love God with ALL your heart - you'll never regret it!"

The race is long and sometimes difficult, but we're definitely not alone. Let's run with perseverance - and when we become discouraged, let's listen for the cheers from the Great Cloud of Witnesses!

STAND ON SOLID GROUND

The gospel message is one of hope. It's a message which says: God loves us and has an eternal plan for our life through His Son Jesus. Without the hope of the gospel, we would continue to sink into the darkness of our sinful desires. Without the hope of the gospel, we would continue to live a life of emptiness and an eternity separated from God.

But as we place our trust in Jesus for the forgiveness of our sin, He lifts us up, gives our life new meaning, and transforms us into a new creation through the power of His Spirit.

Psalm 40:1-2
"I waited patiently for the Lord; He turned to me and heard my cry. He lifted me out of the slimy pit, out of the mud and mire; He set my feet on a rock and gave me a firm place to stand."

These words were written by King David over 1000 years before the death and resurrection of Jesus. And yet, they give us a very good illustration of the hope of the gospel - the message of salvation.

In our sinful nature, we all "have gone astray, each of us has turned to his own way." (Isaiah 53:6). We have all walked down paths which cause us to "fall short of the glory of God." (Romans 3:23). Each of us have been firmly embedded in the mire of sin - and none of us can climb out of the pit with our own strength.

But praise God that before the creation of the world, He had a plan to bring us back to Himself - a plan to rescue us: "While we were still sinners, Christ died for us." (Romans 5:8). The death and resurrection of Jesus allows us victory over sin and creates a way out of the mud: "If you confess with your mouth, 'Jesus is Lord,' and believe in your heart that God raised Him from the dead, you will be saved." (Romans 10:9).

If we truly desire to be clean, we must call out to Jesus as Savior and Lord...today! If we will cry out in faith, He has promised to hear our cry and lift us up. He will give us a life filled with purpose and hope! He will set our feet where we can stand on solid ground.

STAND FIRM

In the message, "Stand On Solid Ground," we related Salvation through faith in Jesus to being "lifted out of the slimy pit, out of the mud and mire." (Psalm 40:2). We saw how God lifts us up and sets our feet upon a rock. But what should we do now that we are standing on solid ground?

When we are in the mud, we're very vulnerable to attack. It's difficult to move and we easily lose our balance. We tend to live in fear, not knowing who to trust or which way to turn. But as we are lifted up, we are washed clean and become "a new creation; the old has gone, the new has come!" (2 Corinthians 5:17).

As the Spirit of God transforms us and makes us new, He gives us everything we need to accomplish His work and live a victorious life: "His divine power has given us everything we need for life and godliness." (2 Peter 1:3). Knowing that our Heavenly Father is working through us, we now have but one "duty" - we must stand!

As the Israelites were approaching the Red Sea, they were consumed with fear because the Egyptian army was rapidly drawing near.

Exodus 14:13

"Moses answered the people, 'Do not be afraid. Stand firm and you will see the deliverance the Lord will bring you today. The Egyptians you see today you will never see again.'"

Before God lifted us out of the pit, He first required us to trust that His Son died for the forgiveness of our sin. If we can trust Him to save us when we are His enemy, how much more should we trust Him to continue to save us now that we have become His child. (Romans 5:10).

Whenever we feel unworthy or unable to accomplish His assigned task - whenever we feel unable to stand - we have begun to look at ourselves rather than focusing on God: "Now it is God who makes both us and you stand firm in Christ." (2 Corinthians 1:21).

We must trust Him to work through us and accomplish what we are unable to do in our own strength. The solid rock is no place to tremble - no place to fear. Our position on the rock is our strength AND our worth. Let's honor our Father as we stand - let's bring Him glory as we stand firm!

OPPORTUNITY TO PRAISE

There are going to be days when we just don't feel like being thankful - we don't seem able to praise. We know we should "rejoice in the Lord always," (Philippians 4:4), and we're trying to learn "the secret of being content in any and every situation," (Philippians 4:12), but sometimes it's just hard.

There are many reasons (or excuses) for days like this. We sometimes lose the eternal perspective of our life and our surroundings. We take our eyes off Jesus and begin to look at the storm (Matthew 14:30). We become excessively entangled in the weeds and are choked off by "the worries of this life and the deceitfulness of wealth." (Matthew 13:22). Or maybe we simply get tired.

Days like this are to be expected. Jesus said, "In this world you will have trouble." (John 16:33) - and our trouble will sometimes strain our relationship with God. But even at this very moment, we are being "transformed into His image." (2 Corinthians 3:18). Even though we may struggle, we are progressing from what we once were to what we will yet become. We are all a work in progress - a work progressing toward the image of Christ.

Psalms 113:3

"From the rising of the sun to the place where it sets, the name of the Lord is to be praised."

We must continue to grow until He is so near that we truly praise Him all day and every day. God deserves praise, He desires praise, and He WILL receive praise!

When Jesus was riding into Jerusalem, crowds of people began to praise Him. Some of the religious leaders in the crowd told Jesus He should make them stop and Jesus responded: "I tell you, if they keep quiet, the stones will cry out." (Luke 19:40).

The Creator of The Universe WILL be praised - one way or the other. Either we offer up our praise or the rocks will begin to sing. No matter what our situation is today let's remember He is worthy! He has picked us up, cleaned us off, and adopted us into His Family. Let's rise up and use this and every other moment of the day to say thank You - let's not miss another opportunity to praise.

EQUIP THE SAINTS

Jesus' ministry on earth lasted only three years, but His message continues to be preached today and has spread to nearly every country and language of the world. When Jesus began His ministry, He knew His time was short. Yet rather than trying to preach to the greatest number of people, Jesus focused the majority of His time on a small group of twelve men.

Jesus taught His disciples about the Kingdom of God and how they must learn to love one another (John 13:34). He taught them about the forgiveness of sin He would provide through His sacrificial death - and He taught them of their need to abide in Him (John 15).

Their intense teaching had one overriding purpose - they were being taught so they could be sent into ministry: "Go and make disciples... teaching them to obey everything I have commanded you." (Matthew 28:19-20). Jesus gave a model for ministry which we should follow today.

Ephesians 4:11-12

"It was He who gave some to be apostles, some to be prophets, some to be evangelists, and some to be pastors and teachers, to prepare God's people for works of service, so that the body of Christ may be built up."

The main purpose of all ministry activity is "to prepare God's people for works of service." The New American Standard Bible renders this verse as "equipping of the saints." We are to ensure that God's people have the necessary tools for ministry.

God has blessed us with His Holy Word. By allowing God's Spirit to minister as we study His Word, our life becomes more at peace and more focused. The purpose of our life becomes clear as we align our priorities with His truth: "Do not store up for yourselves treasures on earth where moth and rust destroy...but store up for yourselves treasures in heaven." (Matthew 6:19-20). The blessings we receive through His Word are not meant to be held - they must be shared: "Freely you have received, freely give." (Matthew 10:8).

My sincere hope is for God to use this ministry to draw each of us into a closer relationship with Himself. But I also pray these messages will help equip us for our ministry to others. In all of our ministry - in our church, work, and family - let's minister with uncompromising truth...and let's always look for ways to equip the saints.

PROVING OUR FAITH

We begin our Christian life in faith: "For it is by grace you have been saved, through faith." (Ephesians 2:8). And as we begin our life in faith, so we must continue to walk in faith: "Just as you received Christ Jesus as Lord, continue to live in Him." (Colossians 2:6). We are to live in Christ the same as we received Him - in faith. We cannot come to Christ without faith and we're unable to live a victorious Christian life without continuously walking in faith.

One of the beautiful truths in God's Kingdom is that everything along our walk has a purpose: "In all things God works for the good of those who love Him." (Romans 8:28). "All things," means even times of hardship and trial. Since faith is such a vital part of our Christian life, many of our trials are for the express purpose of revealing and strengthening our faith.

1 Peter 1:6-7

"For a little while you may have had to suffer grief in all kinds of trials. These have come so that your faith - of greater worth than gold, which perishes even though refined by fire - may be proved genuine."

As hard as it may sometimes be to believe, our trials only last "for a little while." When we view our life on the time scale of eternity, we see our trials as a quick flash. But even these "flashes" of trials have a purpose - "so that your faith...may be proved genuine."

Our faith, which is "of greater worth than gold," must be shown to be real. We must prove our faith not to God, but to ourselves. God already knows the genuineness of our faith. The faith we have is "the measure of faith God has given." (Romans 12:3). But for us to be an effective soldier in His Kingdom - for us to obediently follow - we must clearly see the strength of our own faith.

God will always provide the tools we need, He will always provide the teaching we need, and He will always provide the strengthening we need to accomplish His will. We will emerge from our trials much stronger and much more confident because we will KNOW God is by our side. Let's rejoice that our trials will soon pass - but let's also rejoice that our trials are being used for the purpose of proving our faith.

LIVE BY FAITH

In the message, "Proving Our Faith," we saw how our trials are used to strengthen our faith. We also saw that our faith is revealed to us (made real) as we walk through our trials. An understanding of our faith is necessary to prepare us for the obstacles that eventually cross our path.

We often discuss the importance of faith - and for good reason: "Without faith it is impossible to please God." (Hebrews 11:6). If we desire to live a life pleasing to God, we must learn to live by faith.

2 Corinthians 5:7
"We live by faith and not by sight."

The first step of faith is when we recognize our sinful condition, repent of our sin, and believe Jesus died so our sin can be forgiven. This belief is not a result of what we see, but a result of faith.

As we begin our Christian walk, Jesus becomes more and more real. We begin to "see" Him as we go about our day. Each time our faith is strengthened, our eyes are opened a little wider and we see a little clearer. The challenges of yesterday which required great faith, now only require a comfortable walk...for we now can see!

But we must never mistake the increase of Spiritual sight with the increase of faith. "Now faith is being sure of what we hope for and certain of what we do not see." (Hebrews 11:1). It takes little faith to be sure of what we can see. True faith always involves an assurance of what is unseen.

So what does this mean? If we desire to please God, we must live by faith. If we desire to live by faith, we must continually (again and again) step into the unseen. The unseen is uncomfortable - maybe even a little scary. But stepping into the unseen IS faith...and the only way to please God.

This type of life requires continual fellowship with our Heavenly Father. We must listen very carefully where we should step and be prepared to "trust in the Lord with all your heart and lean not on your own understanding." (Proverbs 3:5). Until the day He calls us Home, we must continue to step and grow - we must continue to live by faith.

CREATE MEMORIALS

After the people of Israel wandered in the desert for 40 years, God led them across the Jordan river into the land of Canaan. This was not an ordinary crossing. God stopped the Jordan river from flowing and allowed the priests to stand in the middle of the river bed with the ark of the covenant as the Israelites walked passed. This event was an obvious miracle that God wanted His people to remember and pass down to future generations.

Joshua 4:5-7

"Each of you is to take up a stone on his shoulder, according to the number of the tribes of the Israelites, to serve as a sign among you. In the future, when your children ask you, 'What do these stones mean?' tell them that the flow of the Jordan was cut off before the ark of the covenant of the Lord. When it crossed the Jordan, the waters of the Jordan were cut off. These stones are to be a memorial to the people of Israel forever.'"

Memorials are anything that remind us of the miraculous work of God. They remind us of those times when God revealed Himself and said: "Let Me show you how much I love you." Without some type of memorial, we tend to forget that God's love and power is real - and available for the asking.

When David went to fight Goliath, he did so without fear because he knew: "The Lord who delivered me from the paw of the lion and the paw of the bear will deliver me from the hand of this Philistine." (1 Samuel 17:37). David had seen God's power and felt His presence during previous battles. It's easy to imagine David with a lion's tooth or a bear claw around his neck as a reminder of God's strength.

We must become more aware of God as He works in our life and in the world around us. As we see and hear Him, we must find ways to create lasting memories for ourselves and those we love. "I will remember the deeds of the Lord; yes, I will remember your miracles of long ago." (Psalm 77:11). Let's never forget He is by our side. Let's help others remember He is in control. Let's share the stories of God's love as we create memorials.

IN HIS COURTS

Once we enter through the gate of Jesus Christ (John 10:9), by believing in Him for the forgiveness of our sins, we have dramatically altered our eternity. We were once blind and destined to be separated from God in Hell, but now we "see" and will spend eternity as His child in Heaven.

After we pass through the Gate, God sets a plan in motion to conform us to the likeness of His Son. (Romans 8:29). God's plan is for us to be transformed into people whose sole desire is to bring Him glory and praise His name forever.

At times, this process can be very painful as we strip away layers of pride and crawl from under the dominion of our old sinful nature. But as we persevere and catch a glimpse of His glory, we will never again desire to be away from His presence.

Psalm 84:10

"Better is one day in Your courts than a thousand elsewhere; I would rather be a doorkeeper in the house of my God than dwell in the tents of the wicked."

A single day in the presence of God is better than a thousand days anywhere else - better than ANYTHING this world can offer. If we do not believe this truth, we have not yet been in His presence - we have not yet tasted the sweet fruit of His Spirit.

Hear the passion in the second part of the above passage: "I would rather be an insignificant doorman in the house of God than reside in the largest mansion while living in wickedness." (My paraphrase). This passion to be in the presence of God is also recorded earlier.

Psalm 84:2

"My soul yearns, even faints, for the courts of the Lord; my heart and my flesh cry out for the living God."

Our Heavenly Father longs for us to have this passion in our life. "Enter His gates with thanksgiving and His courts with praise." (Psalm 100:4). God's holy temple - His place of worship - now resides within every believer....resides within us! (1 Corinthians 3:16). Let's fill His temple with praise - let's passionately spend EVERY day in His courts.

GET ALONE AND PRAY

During Jesus' ministry, He demonstrated complete control over the elements of nature as He "rebuked the wind and the raging waters." (Luke 8:24). He also demonstrated complete control over the human body as He healed the blind, deaf, mute, crippled, leprous, bleeding, demon possessed, and brought the dead to life.

"In the beginning was the Word, and the Word was with God, and the Word was God." (John 1:1). "The Word became flesh and made His dwelling among us." (John 1:14). The words of the Apostle John are clear - Jesus (The Word) is God!

And yet, Jesus lived in human form.

Luke 5:15-16
"The news about Him spread all the more, so the crowds of people came to hear Him and to be healed of their sicknesses. But Jesus often withdrew to lonely places and prayed."

Though He created the Universe, "through Him all things were made," (John 1:3), Jesus still required time alone with the Father. This was time to be refreshed and receive direction. Prior to choosing His twelve apostles, Jesus "went out to a mountainside and spent the night praying." (Luke 6:12). This decision was so important that it required extra time in prayer.

On the night before He was crucified, Jesus was in such anguish that He prayed until "His sweat was like drops of blood falling to the ground." (Luke 22:44). Jesus accepted limitations when He took on human form - and these limitations required dedicated time to talk with the Father.

If the Perfect Man required such time of prayer, how much more necessary is it for us who contain so many flaws. We cannot wave our hand and calm the storm - we must pray and ask for help. We are to live in such communion with God that we "pray continually," (1 Thessalonians 5:17) - even as we drive in busy traffic, manage multiple assignments, or care for noisy children.

But each of us must also set aside time - if not daily, then "often" - where we can withdraw to a quiet place. We all need to be refreshed; we all need clear direction. Let's make sure we set aside time to get alone and pray.

THE BURNING BUSH

Moses was born into slavery as a Hebrew from the tribe of Levi, but circumstances allowed him to be raised as a prince in Pharaoh's court. (Exodus 2:1-10). As a young man, Moses began to see the injustice between the Egyptians and the Hebrews and at one point took matters into his own hands and killed an Egyptian for mistreating a Hebrew slave. This action caused Moses to be misunderstood by the Hebrews and hunted by the Egyptians, so he fled across the desert to the land of Midian and settled down as a shepherd.

Going from an Egyptian prince to a Midianite shepherd was quite a change. As a prince, Moses received the finest education as well as the most advanced military training. However, it was the simple life of a shepherd that truly prepared Moses for God's work.

Moses was a shepherd for 40 years until: "The angel of the Lord appeared to him in flames of fire from within a bush." (Exodus 3:2). Moses had never seen a bush that was on fire but not burning up, so he went to take a closer look.

Exodus 3:4

"When the Lord saw that he had gone over to look, God called to him from within the bush, 'Moses! Moses!' And Moses said, 'Here I am.'"

Notice that God waited until Moses saw the bush, stopped what he was doing, and drew himself near. I wonder how long this bush had been burning before Moses noticed - how long had God been trying to get his attention? During the last 40 years, how many other "burning bushes" had been placed in Moses' path?

"Be still, and know that I am God." (Psalm 46:10). How long had Moses needed to experience the solitude and "stillness" of tending the flock before he was ready to hear God?

God is at work all around us. The bushes are burning, but in the hurriedness of our daily lives we fail to notice - fail to stop and draw near. Is it any wonder we have a hard time hearing from God? God wants to give us clear direction, but He's waiting for us to slow down.

Let's not miss the opportunity to be used by God - to be part of His wonderful plan. Let's create time to be very still - to look intently for where God is working...then with great expectation, let's draw near to the burning bush.

HOLY GROUND

In the message, "The Burning Bush," we saw how God spoke to Moses as he was tending sheep. God used a burning bush to get Moses' attention, and although we don't know for sure, we entertained the possibility that this wasn't the first burning bush along Moses' path.

It's possible God sent several burning bushes to determine when Moses was ready to listen. If we desire to hear from God, we must establish time which is free of distractions - we must be able to see where He is burning and listen for His call.

When Moses approached the bush and heard God call his name, he simply replied: "Here I am." (Exodus 3:4). Moses had no idea how the next few moments would change his life - initially, he didn't even know it was God who called. But God was at work, and Moses' answer signaled his availability. We also must have a heart that daily cries out to God, "Here I am!"

Although Moses drew near and was available, he was not yet ready to listen.

Exodus 3:5

"'Do not come any closer,' God said. 'Take off your sandals, for the place where you are standing is holy ground.'"

Removing the sandals was an act of respect and reverence. Notice that this reverence is not only something we do because God is worthy of our respect - it's something He demands. If we desire to hear His direction, we must bow before Him in reverent and humble submission.

Our relationship with Jesus Christ should produce great assurance. "In Him and through faith in Him we may approach God with freedom and confidence." (Ephesians 3:12). But as we approach the throne, we must remember He is the King and the Creator of ALL things. He has invited us into an intimate relationship, but it must never be a casual event to enter into God's presence.

His presence creates holiness. Without Him, our churches and our homes are nothing but walls and a roof. But as we worship Him with all our heart, His presence resides within us. Each step we take throughout our day must be with reverence for God. Let's remember we are His temple - and we are standing on holy ground.

IT'S ALL ABOUT YOU

In the last two messages, we've looked at Moses' encounter with the burning bush. "Take off your sandals, for the place where you are standing is holy ground." (Exodus 3:5). God had an assignment for Moses that would require complete trust.

God's chosen people (the nation of Israel) had lived in Egypt for 430 years. They arrived as honored guests when Joseph was in charge of the distribution of food. But within a single generation, the people of Israel were forced into slavery and lived under very oppressive conditions.

God chose Moses to be His messenger and instrument of power: "I am sending you to Pharaoh to bring My people the Israelites out of Egypt." (Exodus 3:10). On one hand this was a great honor - on the other, it was very frightening.

Moses gave every possible excuse to convince God He'd made a wrong choice: "Who am I to go to Pharaoh?" (3:11), "What if they do not believe me?" (4:1), "I am slow of speech and tongue." (4:10). God was very patient with Moses, but finally He had enough.

Exodus 4:11-14

"The Lord said to him, 'Who gave man his mouth? Who makes him deaf or mute? Who gives him sight or makes him blind? Is it not I, the Lord? Now go; I will help you speak and will teach you what to say.' But Moses said, 'O Lord, please send someone else to do it.' Then the Lord's anger burned against Moses."

Moses was "more humble than anyone else on the face of the earth." (Numbers 12:2). But in this case, his humility had become a self absorbed lack of faith. Moses looked at his own abilities, and didn't see how success was possible. He failed to see the Creator of the Universe who promised to walk by His side.

Our Christian walk is ALL about God working through us. Of course the tasks will seem impossible. Our Heavenly Father desires an intimate relationship - why would He lead us in a direction that did not require His help? But His call is our greatest assurance of victory. "If God be for us, who can be against us." (Romans 8:31).

When God is truly Lord of our life, it's false humility to believe we cannot follow where He leads. Let's allow His glory to so completely fill our vision that we can boldly say, 'I can follow because I KNOW....it's all about You.'

MOVE ON

Moses received clear instruction as God spoke to him from the burning bush: "I am sending you to Pharaoh to bring My people the Israelites out of Egypt." (Exodus 3:10). Moses debated with God regarding his assignment and pushed God to the limit of His patience: "The Lord's anger burned against Moses." (Exodus 4:14).

But once he began to follow, Moses maintained a very close relationship with God and was a first-hand witness to many miracles. God worked through Moses to bring plagues against the Egyptians and to miraculously bring the Israelites out of Egypt. As their journey into the desert began, Moses witnessed more of God's power: "By day the Lord went ahead of them in a pillar of cloud to guide them on their way and by night in a pillar of fire to give them light." (Exodus 13:21).

As the Israelites approached the Red Sea, Pharaoh sent every chariot in Egypt to bring the Israelites back. With no escape route in sight and the Egyptian army closing in, Moses cried out to God.

Exodus 14:15-16
"Then the Lord said to Moses, 'Why are you crying out to Me? Tell the Israelites to move on. Raise your staff and stretch out your hand over the sea to divide the water so that the Israelites can go through the sea on dry ground.'"

God had been in close communion with Moses. He had given His direction and demonstrated His awesome power. Now at this moment of crisis, God expected Moses to know what to do: "Why are you crying out to Me...move on."

We must always create time to "be still and know that He is God." (Psalm 46:10). But we cannot allow our waiting to make us immobile. "Whoever watches the wind will not plant; whoever looks at the clouds will not reap." (Ecclesiastes 11:4). The conditions will never be perfect and we will never feel fully prepared, but "if God is for us, who can be against us?" (Romans 8:31).

There will always come a time when God expects us to demonstrate our faith in what He has provided. Let's prepare for that time by drawing near and learning to trust in HIS ability. Let's live with an active faith such that when His direction is clear, we are able to move on.

HOLD UP THEIR ARMS

The Amalekites were attacking Moses and the people of Israel. The Israelites did not have the power to win this battle on their own, so Moses sent Joshua to the battlefield and then climbed to the top of a hill: "I will stand on top of the hill with the staff of God in my hands." (Exodus 17:9).

God had previously demonstrated His power by using Moses and this same staff to part the Red Sea (Exodus 14:16), and cause water to flow out of a rock (Exodus 17:5-6). Moses was now trusting God to demonstrate His power once again through this staff as he lifted his hands.

Exodus 17:11-13
"As long as Moses held up his hands, the Israelites were winning, but whenever he lowered his hands, the Amalekites were winning. When Moses' hands grew tired, they took a stone and put it under him and he sat on it. Aaron and Hur held his hands up - one on one side, one on the other - so that his hands remained steady till sunset. So Joshua overcame the Amalekite army with the sword."

Moses knew what he had to do, but he simply became worn out. Fortunately for the people of Israel, Moses had two trusted companions who stood by his side and were willing to hold up his arms in battle.

The world is in desperate need of many more like Moses and Joshua - those who are willing to lead and fight on the front lines. But we are literally starving for more like Aaron and Hur. We must be prepared to stand beside our friends and leaders when the battle is raging and hold up their arms.

Who is the "Moses" in our life? Who is in need of extra encouragement? "But encourage one another daily, as long as it is called Today, so that none of you may be hardened by sin's deceitfulness." (Hebrews 3:13). Our pastors, teachers, and ministry leaders may appear strong - but their arms are getting very tired. Our missionaries have great faith, but they are also very lonely.

Our Brothers and Sisters are in a battle today. Let's be a continual source of encouragement - let's be like Aaron or Hur and hold up their arms!

WATCH FOR HIS RETURN

There will always be a fascination with the end times. There will be those who study every detail of scripture in an attempt to pinpoint a date and those who simply feel the end is near because of our current moral decay.

Questions concerning the end times are not new. Two thousand years ago, the disciples asked Jesus: "What will be the signs of Your coming and of the end of the age?" (Matthew 24:3). Jesus answered the question directly and in several parables, but His basic message was: "You also must be ready, because the Son of Man will come at an hour when you do not expect Him." (Matthew 24:44).

There's nothing wrong with discussing the end times. The return of Jesus Christ is our "blessed hope." (Titus 2:13). But we should never allow our discussions to cause argument or division. (2 Timothy 2:23). I've studied the end times fairly well and the one thing I can say with absolute certainty is: "He's coming back!"

Mark 13:35-37
"Therefore keep watch because you do not know when the owner of the house will come back - whether in the evening, or at midnight, or when the rooster crows, or at dawn. If he comes suddenly, do not let him find you sleeping. What I say to you, I say to everyone: 'Watch!'"

Are we ready for the Owner of the House to return? We can't afford to wait for that next promotion or for the kids to grow - we must be prepared today. If the end of our time on earth were to occur tomorrow, did our thoughts, words, and deeds for today bring glory and honor to our Heavenly Father? If the answer is no, we need to do some changing - we need to wake up and clean house. For what is the purpose of breathing if not to bring Him glory?

The study and discussion of end times should cause us to praise God for His victory over evil. Our understanding of the end times should cause us to walk in reverent obedience and help us fight the pulls of the world. Let's not be caught sleeping. Rather, let's look forward with great anticipation and commit to being prepared. Let's draw near to our Lord in prayer and watch for His return.

EVIDENCE OF GOD

It's natural to want to see a clear sign from God. We tell ourselves that if God would give us signs like He gave Moses or Abraham, then all doubt would be removed. But Paul reminds us that all creation is a sign - the Universe in all its wonderful splendor is evidence of a masterful Creator.

Romans 1:20

"For since the creation of the world God's invisible qualities - His eternal power and divine nature - have been clearly seen, being understood from what has been made, so that men are without excuse."

There are clear signs of God all around us - we are all "without excuse!" We cry out for evidence, and yet we see, hear, smell, touch, and taste evidence every day - He is here! And just as the quality of a watch indicates the skill of the watchmaker, so the infinite detail and beauty of creation indicates the "eternal power and divine nature" of the Creator.

It's not surprising that the world does not recognize the evidence: "the sinful mind is hostile to God." (Romans 8:7). The world lives in darkness and is blind to the wonders of our Heavenly Father. But we no longer belong to the world.

If we have truly been "rescued from the dominion of darkness," (Colossians 1:13), through faith in Jesus Christ, we must begin to live according to the Light. We have received the Spirit of Christ and must now learn to submit to the Spirit's control. The Spirit will guide us in every step and every decision. The Spirit will also allow us to clearly see and hear.

God is calling us into a continual fellowship with Himself: "Rejoice in the Lord ALWAYS!" (Philippians 4:4). "Pray continually!" (1 Thessalonians 5:17). To constantly rejoice and pray, we must see God in the flowers, trees, and stars - we must hear Him when the bird sings or the baby cries.

Let's worship Him every moment of every day! Let's submit to the Spirit and open our senses to the evidence of God.

THE FATHER'S VIEW

Have you ever watched ants as they build their home? They scurry about frantically moving little grains of sand from here to there. If we could ask an ant to describe his world, he might tell us about his hole in the ground, about the few hundred members of his family, and maybe something about the few surrounding meters where he gathers food. From our perspective, the ant's view is very limited.

As our Heavenly Father watches us build our homes - frantically moving from here to there - He wants us to always remember: "As the heavens are higher than the earth, so are My ways higher than your ways and My thoughts than your thoughts." (Isaiah 55:9). From God's perspective, our view is VERY limited. God wants to lead us to the place where, even though we may not understand, we trust.

Proverbs 3:5-6
"Trust in the Lord with all your heart and lean not on your own understanding; in all your ways acknowledge Him, and He will make your paths straight."

Many of us are facing difficult decisions. We want to walk along God's path, but we're not sure which direction to turn. We must learn to look at our circumstances through the eye's of God and trust Him with all our heart. Only then will our path be made clear and straight.

Our Father loves us so much that He sent Jesus to die for our sins. He was willing to sacrifice ALL so we could have the opportunity to truly worship Him. All our good times, bad times, joys, and sorrows - all our peaks and all our valleys - work together for the good (Romans 8:28). ALL things work together to conform us "to the likeness of His Son," (Romans 8:29), and draw us toward a closer walk with our Lord.

Our Father knows, sees, and hears ALL. We are fortunate to see a few short steps down the path, but God sees the entire journey. We must learn to lean on Him, continually seek His direction, and trust the Father's view.

TO COMPLETION

There are two great tragedies within the Christian faith today. The first is that many who think they are on their way to Heaven will one day find they are sadly mistaken. This tragedy must be fought by speaking the truth about Salvation. We must teach of the need to trust in the saving grace offered through the sacrifice of Jesus Christ for the forgiveness of sin. We must teach that faith in Jesus is the ONLY way to spend eternity in Heaven.

The second great tragedy is that many who have truly trusted in Jesus for the forgiveness of sin, will live their earthly days full of doubt and fear. We must also fight this tragedy by speaking the truth about Salvation. Many who are on their way to Heaven begin to doubt when they don't feel worthy or "good enough" to deserve such a gift. But the truth is that none of us are good enough! "For all have sinned and fall short of the glory of God." (Romans 3:23).

No one will enter Heaven based on what they have done - only on whom they have placed their faith. "For it is by grace you have been saved, through faith." (Ephesians 2:8). At the moment of Salvation, we become an eternal Child of God: "You are not your own; you were bought at a price." (1 Corinthians 6:19-20). We were purchased with the blood of Jesus and have become a "new creation: the old has gone, the new has come." (2 Corinthians 5:17).

We are "born again" as a new creation. And as a new creation, we must learn to crawl and then walk. We may sometimes stumble, but God promises we will continue to grow.

Philippians 1:6
"Being confident of this, that He who began a good work in you will carry it on to completion until the day of Christ Jesus."

On the day of our Salvation, God began His work in us. He gave us His Holy Spirit and "sealed {us} for the day of redemption." (Ephesians 4:30). His wonderful plan is for us to be "conformed to the likeness of His Son." (Romans 8:29). Be confident in God's promise. He WILL finish His work - He WILL carry it on to completion.

WHOM WE WILL SERVE

Joshua led the people of Israel into the promised land of Canaan and helped them fight many battles. Toward the end of his life, Joshua gathered the leaders of Israel for some final encouragement: "You yourselves have seen everything the Lord your God has done to all these nations for your sake; it was the Lord your God who fought for you." (Joshua 23:3).

Joshua wanted the leaders to know that God would continue to fight for them - but also, that God expected obedience to His Word: "If you violate the covenant of the Lord your God, and go and serve other gods and bow down to them, the Lord's anger will burn against you." (Joshua 23:16). He then gathered all the people and told them the time had come to make a choice.

Joshua 24:15

"But if serving the Lord seems undesirable to you, then choose for yourselves this day whom you will serve, whether the gods your forefathers served beyond the river, or the gods of the Amorites, in whose land you are living. But as for me and my household, we will serve the Lord."

The Israelites had seen God's mighty hand - the time had now come to make a decision. They would either serve the Lord with ALL their heart, or serve the man made gods of the world.

We face the same decision today. We either decide to follow and serve Jesus, or we have decided to serve the priorities and "gods" of this world. "Whoever believes in Him is not condemned, but whoever does not believe stands condemned already because he has not believed in the name of God's one and only Son." (John 3:18).

Notice that Joshua boldly spoke for his entire home: "WE will serve the Lord!" Everyone must make their own decision about Jesus, but each of us have a wonderful opportunity to influence others - especially those in our family.

There is no longer a middle road. We must once and for all decide to serve our Lord and Savior. Today, we must choose whom we will serve.

LOOKING AT THE HEART

The nation of Israel was ruled by judges for over 300 years. The people then cried out for a king: "Then we will be like the other nations." (1 Samuel 8:20). God gave them what they wanted - He gave them Saul: "An impressive young man without equal among the Israelites." (1 Samuel 9:2).

Saul was an impressive looking king, but he failed to obey God's instructions. Therefore, God rejected Saul as king and sent Samuel to anoint a new king from amongst the sons of Jesse. When Samuel arrived at Jesse's home, he saw Eliab and thought for sure he was to be the next king.

1 Samuel 16:7

"But the Lord said to Samuel, 'Do not consider his appearance or his height, for I have rejected him. The Lord does not look at the things man looks at. Man looks at the outward appearance, but the Lord looks at the heart.'"

Saul was the type of king the people desired and Samuel assumed the next king would fit into this same "impressive" mold - but this king would be chosen according to God's criteria. David would be chosen based on the condition of his heart.

How much time and effort do we expend on the external features of our life? How much of our life is concerned with being externally "impressive?" Let's take a moment to allow the Word to cut deep and honestly evaluate our priorities. God doesn't look at the external parts of our life - He looks intently at our heart. "Create in me a pure heart, O God." (Psalm 51:10).

There are very few things in life which have eternal value. And NOTHING outside of God's Will can survive the flames of judgement. The priorities that occupy our life become our treasure - and our treasure defines our heart: "Where your treasure is, there your heart will be also." (Matthew 6:21).

Let's refocus our time and energy. Let's spend less on becoming "impressive" in the eyes of the world, and more on storing up "treasures in heaven." (Matthew 6:20). God's judgement is the only one that will ever matter - and He's looking at the heart.

SET THE EXAMPLE

When Paul sent his letters to the Corinthians, the gospel accounts of Jesus had not yet been written. Most believers didn't know many of the details of Jesus' life, so it was difficult to encourage people by saying to live as Jesus would live. Instead, Paul led others to Jesus through the example he demonstrated in his own life.

1 Corinthians 11:1
"Follow my example, as I follow the example of Christ."

Paul certainly didn't claim to be perfect. He would be the first to stand up and say: "What a wretched man I am!" (Romans 7:24). Though Paul wrote and preached on how to live the Christian life, he still admitted his imperfections. "Not that I have already obtained all this, or have been made perfect, but I press on to take hold of that which Christ Jesus took hold of me." (Philippians 3:12).

And yet, Paul also knew he was a child of God and was willing to place his life in open view for others to examine and imitate: "Whatever you have learned or received or heard from me, or seen in me - put it into practice." (Philippians 4:9).

When we claim to follow Jesus, the world takes notice - like it or not. We may not feel we are witnessing, but for many people we're the only view of Jesus they will ever see - the only words of Jesus they will ever hear. We may not realize it, but the way we live cries out, "Follow my example, as I follow the example of Christ."

Do we set an example for others to follow? Would our example cause others to be drawn closer to God or to drift further away? Do we follow Jesus' command to love one another, so that: "By this all men will know you are My disciples." (John 13:35).

This is a huge responsibility. A good friend of mine had an "I Love Jesus" sticker on the back of his car. One day he became convicted by his driving habits. He realized that his driving was not setting a very good example. His solution to this "dilemma" was to remove the sticker.

We cannot remove the "I Love Jesus" sticker from our lives. The world is watching and we must be bold enough to stand and accept the accountability. We need men and women of strength and character - Brothers and Sisters who love one another and love the Lord with all their heart, soul, mind, and strength! I urge you to be among those who commit to live a life that brings glory and honor to God in ALL you do - be bold and set the example.

FREE OF THORNS

In the parable of the sower (Matthew 13:3-8), Jesus tells about a farmer who scatters seed on four different types of soil - packed, shallow, thorny, and fertile. In this parable, the seed refers to the Word of God and the soil refers to those who hear the Word.

Most of us fall into one of the last two types of soil. We desire God's Word to grow on fertile ground and produce a bountiful crop, but we seem to continually battle the thorns.

Matthew 13:22

"The one who received the seed that fell among the thorns is the man who hears the Word, but the worries of this life and the deceitfulness of wealth choke it, making it unfruitful."

We have more opportunity to hear God's Word today than at any other time in history. We can hear good preaching in church, on radio, on tape, or over the internet. We can read God's Word in a variety of Bible translations, and receive an abundance of help with interpretation through commentaries, dictionaries, and devotionals. Our soil is definitely receiving seed. But the challenge is to keep our lives free of the distractions which hinder the seed's growth.

Here's a simple test of our soil. Jesus said the number one commandment is to "Love the Lord your God with all your heart and with all your soul and with all your mind." (Matthew 22:37). When was the last time our heart overflowed with love for God? When was the last time we thought about Jesus and nearly bubbled over with: "Thank You!"

God wants us to love Him. If we have a hard time with this most basic command, it's no wonder we're confused about where He's leading us. When God's Word comes into our life, we should receive it as a precious gift and look for immediate ways to apply it and make it grow - not process it through the distractions of deadlines, appointments, bills, and worldly pursuits.

Is the Word growing in our life, or is it being choked by unnecessary demands of the world? "The world and its desires pass away," (1 John 2:17), but the things of God are eternal. It's time for some internal gardening - it's time to remove distractions so the seed of His Word can grow and bear fruit. God is calling us to live a life dedicated to Him - a life of consistent faith in ALL we do. Let's begin by developing fertile soil which is free of thorns.

CUT THE LIFEBOATS

At the end of his third missionary journey, Paul was arrested in Jerusalem, transferred about 40 miles up the road to Caesarea, and sat in prison for over two years before being sent by boat to stand trial in Rome. During the journey to Rome, a storm blew the ship off course and threatened to kill everyone on board.

Acts 27:30-32

"In an attempt to escape from the ship, the sailors let the lifeboat down into the sea, pretending they were going to lower some anchors from the bow. Then Paul said to the centurion and the soldiers, 'Unless these men stay with the ship, you cannot be saved.' So the soldiers cut the ropes that held the lifeboat and let it fall away."

Most of us have lifeboats which we keep close to our side. Even after we've accepted the forgiveness and saving grace of Jesus, we tend to keep the lifeboats - just in case. We say we're trusting our future to God, but we still make sure every step of our life is planned for the next 30 years - just in case.

We say we understand the concept of eternity and the idea that our life is "a mist that appears for a little while and then vanishes," (James 4:14), but we still want our friends and family to remember us as "successful" - just in case. We say we want to live for Jesus, but we still don't want to miss the pleasures of the world - just in case.

If we keep one foot in the ship and one foot in the lifeboat, we will never live as God desires. It makes absolutely no sense to say we believe and trust God with our eternity and yet fail to trust Him with the uncertainties of tomorrow or the storms of today. Cutting the lifeboats means we place ALL our trust in God, believe His Word as truth, and live accordingly - "Do not merely listen to the Word, and so deceive yourselves. Do what it says." (James 1:22).

Ask God to reveal any area of your life which is not consistent with a life of belief and trust. Then ask for the strength and courage to cut the lifeboats.

BEGIN WITH REJOICING

In his letter to the Philippians, Paul gives an exhortation to "Rejoice in the Lord always - and again I say, rejoice!" (Philippians 4:4). Paul had been arrested and sent to Rome to await trial. He now spent his days and nights chained to a Roman soldier, but he was still able to say, rejoice....always!

When we begin to grasp the life changing gift of forgiveness through faith in the sacrifice of Jesus; when we realize that eternity lasts a very, VERY long time; and when we truly believe that our eternity will be spent in the presence of the Lord, we should have reason to rejoice no matter what our present circumstances might be. The verses which immediately follow Paul's call to rejoice list some very real benefits of a life of rejoicing.

Philippians 4:5-7
> *"Let your gentleness be evident to all. The Lord is near. Do not be anxious about anything, but in everything, by prayer and petition, with thanksgiving, present your requests to God. And the peace of God, which transcends all understanding, will guard your hearts and your minds in Christ Jesus."*

Gentleness and a lack of anxiety result from rejoicing in a risen Savior. If Jesus Christ can raise from the dead and sit down "at the right hand of God," (Hebrews 10:12), then ALL things are truly possible. If God can speak the Heavens and the Earth into existence, He can take care of the problems with our job, health, kids, finances or relationship - so rejoice! When we rejoice because of an eternity in Heaven, our anxiety fades - our trials become "light and momentary." (2 Corinthians 4:17).

By living a life filled with rejoicing, we take our eyes off the problems of the world and focus on the solutions of God. We develop a heart of thanksgiving - a heart which naturally presents everything to God in prayer and waits with grateful expectation for His reply. We begin to trust in God's plan for our life and His desire for us to be with Him forever. The final result is "the peace of God which transcends all understanding."

Does this sounds like a great way to live? God offers a life of gentleness, contentment, and peace to all of His children - but we must begin with rejoicing.

DEDICATE THE TEMPLE

The Old Testament adds wonderful richness to our faith. From the earliest writings, we read of the creation of the heavens and the earth. We gain great confidence as we see God use common men and women to accomplish His purpose - even though these common people had many of our same flaws. The Old Testament also provides a clear picture of a chosen people (the nation of Israel) being taught to worship and live in absolute reverence of the Lord.

After the Israelites were led out of Egypt, God gave instructions to Moses for constructing the Tabernacle. The Tabernacle was made of cloth, animal skins, and poles so it could be easily moved. This was to be the central place of worship and where the presence of God would reside.

After several hundred years, the people of Israel settled into the promised land. God gave King David the vision for a permanent Temple which would replace the mobile Tabernacle. David made plans and collected material, but God waited for Solomon to become king before construction began.

It took Solomon seven years to construct the Temple using over 150,000 workers. (2 Chronicles 2:1-2). When the Temple was complete, the dedication began. Sacrifices were made to honor and worship God. Music was played and songs were sung "to give praise and thanks to the Lord." (2 Chronicles 5:13).

2 Chronicles 5:13-14
"Then the Temple of the Lord was filled with a cloud, and the priests could not perform their service because of the cloud, for the glory of the Lord filled the Temple of God."

One thousand years after the Temple was dedicated, Jesus died on the cross and we entered into a new covenant with a new Temple: "Don't you know that you yourselves are God's Temple and that God's Spirit lives in you?" (1 Corinthians 3:16).

WE are now the Temple of God. The plans have been developed and the construction is complete - the time has now come for dedication. We must honor Him as Lord and set aside our lives as a holy place for worship (Romans 12:1). As our love and worship becomes focused on God, we will no longer perform "our" service. Everything we do will become His because our lives will be filled with the glory of the Lord. It's time to dedicate the Temple.

EVER-INCREASING GLORY

In the message, "Dedicate The Temple," we saw that through the forgiveness of Jesus and the indwelling of the Holy Spirit, we are now God's Temple. "Don't you know that you yourselves are God's Temple and that God's Spirit lives in you?" (1 Corinthians 3:16). And as with the Temple during the reign of King Solomon, we are to dedicate ourselves for worship and be filled with His glory. (2 Chronicles 5:13-14).

The glory of the Lord first appeared to the people of Israel after they were led out of Egypt: "They looked toward the desert, and there was the glory of the Lord appearing in the cloud." (Exodus 16:10). Then, when Moses was called up Mount Sinai to receive the law, the glory of the Lord settled over the mountain: "To the Israelites the glory of the Lord looked like a consuming fire." (Exodus 24:17).

When Moses came down from the mountain, "his face was radiant because he had spoken with the Lord." (Exodus 34:29). The people were afraid to look upon this reflection of God's glory, so Moses placed a veil over his face. (Exodus 34:33).

These examples of God's glory give us a sense of awe. God's glory encompasses His character - His majesty, holiness, and awesome power. As believers in Jesus Christ, we are now God's Temple and are called to reflect His glory into the world. We are no longer like Moses who had to cover his face with a veil. Jesus has removed the veil and we should now BOLDLY reflect His glory.

2 Corinthians 3:18
"And we, who with unveiled faces all reflect the Lord's glory, are being transformed into His likeness with ever-increasing glory."

When we accept Jesus as our Lord and Savior, we begin the process of being transformed into the image of Christ. We will never attain the full likeness of Christ until we join Him in Heaven, but with every step along God's path, we become more and more like His Son.

We must continue down His path. We must take daily steps toward a life which reflects the glory of the Lord into the darkness that surrounds us. Heavenly Father, may our lives reflect You with an ever-increasing glory.

ENTER HIS REST

The last two messages have considered aspects of the glory of the Lord. We saw how we are God's Temple and are to reflect an "ever-increasing" amount of His glory into the world as we are transformed into the likeness of Christ. (2 Corinthians 3:18).

We reflect the ever-increasing glory of the Lord as we allow the fruit of His Spirit to be more and more evident in our life. As we allow "love, joy, peace, patience, kindness, goodness, faithfulness, gentleness, and self control," (Galatians 5:22-23), to be the defining character of our life, God's glory will shine.

It's clear that our lives ought to produce an abundance of Spiritual fruit. But how? Where should we concentrate our effort in the process of fruit production?

Hebrews 4:10-11
"For anyone who enters God's rest also rests from his own work, just as God did from His. Let us, therefore, make every effort to enter that rest."

The first chapter of Genesis describes how God created the heavens and the earth in six days. "By the seventh day God had finished the work He had been doing; so on the seventh day he rested from all His work." (Genesis 2:2).

God did not begin His work again on the eighth day. He was satisfied and entered into His rest for eternity. "His work has been finished since the creation of the world." (Hebrews 4:3). God is still involved in our lives, but He accomplishes everything from a position of rest - He KNOWS the final outcome.

Likewise, we must not cease from "doing" the things God calls us to do, but we must cease from "working" in our own strength. We know what Spiritual fruit looks like and we should continually guide our steps in that direction. But God is in complete control and we are to place all of our effort in loving Him: "If a man remains in Me and I in him, he will bear much fruit; apart from Me you can do nothing." (John 15:5).

Fruit produced in our own strength is nothing but a cheap and tasteless imitation. We must cling to the vine of Jesus and allow the glory of God to flow through us. Our lives will reflect His glory and produce His fruit only as we make every effort to remain in Him and enter His rest.

GOD MAKES IT GROW

Paul wrote his first letter to the Corinthian church to correct several problems. The Corinthian's needed instruction in marriage, Christian freedom, worship, and various issues which tended to cause division.

Paul rebuked the church for quarreling about being a follower of Paul or a follower of Apollos. Apollos was a good teacher, but Paul reminded the Corinthians (and us) that all ministers of the Gospel are simply servants through whom God accomplishes His work. In the end, the only one worth "following" is Jesus.

1 Corinthians 3:5-6
"What, after all, is Apollos? And what is Paul? Only servants, through whom you came to believe - as the Lord has assigned to each his task. I planted the seed, Apollos watered it, but God made it grow."

We are all given tasks to carry out in the lives of those around us. God desires us to plant the seed of His Word and water with discipleship, prayer, and encouragement. He will then use us to draw others into a saving relationship with Jesus Christ and grow His children into the likeness of His Son.

As we plant and water into the lives of others, it's normal to want (and even expect) to see growth. We may desire to see blossoms overnight, but God is in charge of the growth rate. He is not growing a flower that looks good today but quickly withers away, He is growing a mighty shade tree with deep roots and wide branches that will not break in the wind. And this kind of growth takes time.

No one plants an acorn thinking they will sit under the shade of a mighty oak next month or even next year. Acorns are planted so our children, grandchildren, and even great grandchildren will have shade. What we plant and water today in God's Kingdom may grow slowly, but it may also provide much needed shade for many generations.

We may never see the results of our effort, but we must patiently continue to plant and water. We must learn to recognize the needs of those God places in our path and effectively minister at every opportunity. We must not become discouraged. God has called us to this task and we must obediently follow. We are to plant and water - but always remember, God makes it grow.

STRONG, COURAGEOUS, AND HUMBLE

Joshua was Moses' field commander in the fight against the Amalekites (Exodus 17:9) and his assistant when the Law was given at Mount Sinai (Exodus 24:13).

After exploring the land of Canaan, Joshua was one of only two men to advise the Israelites to trust God and enter the Promised Land. (Numbers 14:6-9). When the people refused, Joshua received an additional 39 years of training under Moses while the Israelites wandered through the desert. With all this preparation, Joshua was the natural successor of Moses (Numbers 27:18-20).

After the death of Moses, God gave final instructions to Joshua before leading the people into the land of Canaan. Joshua would need to be a mighty warrior in the days ahead so God told him three times within four verses to "Be strong and courageous!" (Joshua 1:6-9).

Joshua 1:9

"Have I not commanded you? Be strong and courageous. Do not be terrified; do not be discouraged, for the Lord your God will be with you wherever you go."

This is an awesome exhortation for us today. God has given us His instructions and has told us to boldly proceed down His path - knowing that He is by our side wherever we go. But we have an additional lesson to learn.

Prior to his first battle in Canaan, Joshua "saw a man standing in front of him with a drawn sword in his hand." (Joshua 5:13). This caused Joshua some obvious concern, so he approached the man and asked: "Are you for us or for our enemies?"

Joshua 5:14

" 'Neither,' he replied, 'but as commander of the army of the Lord I have now come.' Then Joshua fell facedown to the ground in reverence, and asked him, 'What message does my Lord have for his servant?' "

Our boldness will always become self serving unless we totally submit to God's leadership - unless we humbly say: "Lord, You are the commander. This is Your army. I will fight with courage and strength, but these are Your battles. What would You have me do, where would You have me go?" As we go forward into God's Land of Promise, our marching orders are to be strong, courageous, and humble.

GIVE THOUGHT TO OUR WAYS

The motivational speakers of our day want us to set great goals for our life. Where do we want to be in 5 years? - in 10 years? What type of lifestyle do we want when we are 65? We are encouraged to set goals which are beyond what we think we can reach - then we are to create a plan to accomplish these goals.

While there's nothing wrong with setting goals and creating plans, we must first ask a longer term question. We must first ask: "Where do we want to be in 100 years?" Until we grasp the significance of this question and have a solid answer, the rest of our goals will be based on a false set of criteria and are not worth pursuing. What difference does it make which college we attend or which job we take or what our home looks like if we have failed to address the issue of where we will spend eternity!?

Proverbs 14:8
"The wisdom of the prudent is to give thought to their ways, but the folly of fools is deception."

Do not be deceived! Even though the average life span continues to increase, life is still short. An average life lasts about 45,000,000 minutes. This seem like a lot, but by this time tomorrow, 1440 minutes will be gone - and 100 years from now.... "You are a mist that appears for a little while and then vanishes." (James 4:14).

Ephesians 5:15-16
"Be very careful, then, how you live - not as unwise but as wise, making the most of every opportunity, because the days are evil."

Each minute of our life is a precious gift from God. We must not waste these gifts by chasing after things which vanish. We MUST learn to evaluate all our decisions and goals based on the overriding goal of living a life dedicated to God - of spending an eternity worshiping Him in Heaven. The clock continues to tick - let's give thought to our ways!

GREAT EXPECTATIONS

Paul was in a Roman prison when he wrote his letter to the Philippians. He didn't know whether he would be set free or executed - but he knew Jesus Christ as his Lord and Savior. Paul had seen God's hand at work and fully understood His love and power. He had completely turned his life over to God and now lived with great expectations of how God would use him to accomplish His plan.

Philippians 1:20

"I eagerly expect and hope that I will in no way be ashamed, but will have sufficient courage so that now as always Christ will be exalted in my body whether by life or by death."

Paul's situation may have appeared dismal and without hope, but he had already seen how God was using ALL things to His glory. "It has become clear throughout the whole palace guard and to everyone else that I am in chains for Christ." (Philippians 1:13). Paul's hardship had made it possible for the whole palace guard to hear the gospel message and had encouraged others to "speak the word of God more courageously and fearlessly." (Philippians 1:14).

As we follow Jesus and learn of God's character through His Word - as we communicate with Him in prayer and place all of our trust in Him - we must develop a view which is not constrained by what we see: "For what is seen is temporary, but what is unseen is eternal." (2 Corinthians 4:18).

An eternal view allows us to see everything in our life as working together for the good. Though the "world's view" of our situation may seem bleak, an eternal view will see God using our daily trials to draw us closer to Him. When our schedule and goals are interrupted, an eternal view allows us to adjust our priorities and see the opportunity for ministry. Jesus was able to "endure the cross" because He could look past the present pain to a time of great joy. (Hebrews 12:2).

Every day God presents us with many opportunities to know Him better. He also places people in our path who need to be encouraged - who need to know of His love. Let's develop a view which "expectantly" looks for these opportunities. Let's begin each day in wondrous anticipation: "I can't wait to see what God has planned for me today!" God is doing an amazing work through the lives of His children. Let's live as we believe and live our lives with great expectations.

A TEMPLE WITH ETERNAL VALUE

In 586 B.C., the armies of Babylon destroyed the Temple in Jerusalem. About 50 years later, the Jewish people began to rebuild. But after a few short years, their priorities began to shift. Suddenly, the condition of their own homes became more important than being obedient to God's call: "Is it time for you yourselves to be living in your paneled houses, while this house {of the Lord} remains a ruin?" (Haggai 1:4). God sent a message through the prophet Haggai which challenged the people to reconsider their values and return to the work they had begun.

Haggai 1:5-6

"Now this is what the Lord Almighty says: 'Give careful thought to your ways. You have planted much, but have harvested little. You eat, but never have enough. You drink, but never have your fill. You put on clothes, but are not warm. You earn wages, only to put them in a purse with holes in it.'"

The people of Israel had turned their attention from rebuilding the Temple to building their own homes - from rebuilding their Spiritual lives to building their physical lives - and found that no matter how hard they worked, they never had enough.

We have more pulls on our priorities today than at any other time in history. There are more distractions and definitely more temptations. We must take a hard look at where we concentrate our time and energy. If our focus is on building for today, we will also be ones who find we never have enough. All our effort will drain through the holes at the bottom of the purse.

We must continue to build - but we must build with our eyes on eternity. We must build the foundation through times of intimate prayer. We must erect the walls through the daily reading His Word. And we must cover what we build with an overriding desire to love God "with all your heart and with all your soul and with all your mind and with all your strength." (Mark 12:30). Each and every day we are building His Temple. Let's evaluate our priorities and begin building a Temple with eternal value.

WITH ALL OUR HEART

The people of Israel had rebelled against God. Despite numerous warnings from the prophet Jeremiah, they refused to change. God's punishment was for many Israelites to be killed in battle and the survivors taken into captivity for seventy years by the Babylonians. Yet even during this time of severe discipline, God demonstrated His compassion and mercy.

Jeremiah 29:10-13

"'When seventy years are completed for Babylon, I will come to you and fulfill My gracious promise to bring you back to this place. For I know the plans I have for you,' declares the Lord, 'plans to prosper you and not to harm you, plans to give you hope and a future. Then you will call upon Me and come and pray to Me, and I will listen to you. You will seek Me and find Me when you seek Me with all your heart.'"

Despite the required discipline, God said His promise would be fulfilled. However, His promise had a condition. God gave the same condition He had always given: You will be blessed if you give Me ALL your heart - if you worship Me and obey My commands.

It's God's desire to bring us out of the captivity of sin and into the freedom of Holy fellowship with Him. His plan is for us to have a life of joy where our hearts are filled with worship regardless of our physical surroundings or circumstances. This type of worship cannot be found in our spare time or in the last few moments before we go to sleep. It must be the all consuming top priority of our day - literally the top priority of our life.

I have a friend in England who is confined to a wheelchair. She has a variety of physical ailments which cause her great discomfort throughout the day. The doctors recently informed her she may have a fatal illness. Yet, when I asked her number one prayer request, she said to pray that her relationship with God would remain close and strong. More important than healing - more cherished than comfort - she valued being near to God.

Do we desire "the peace of God which transcends all understanding?" (Philippians 4:7). We must call upon Him. Do we desire the contentment which remains stable "in any and every situation?" (Philippians 4:12). We must pray to Him...and pray continually. Do we want to know God's perfect plan for our life - do we really want to find Him? We must seek Him - but we must seek Him with all our heart!

THE DESIRES OF OUR HEART

God is The Creator of "the heavens and the earth." (Genesis 1:1). Through Jesus Christ, "all things were made; without Him nothing was made that has been made." (John 1:3). When God created man, He made us "in His own image." (Genesis 1:27). One of the conflicts this establishes is in our tendency to want to create.

Our creative nature is a wonderful gift. We have the ability to think complex and abstract thoughts. New styles of music, art, and literature as well as advances in technology and medicine are all due to our gift of creativity. But all too often, we use this gift to shape and "create" a world around us which conforms to our plans and fulfills our desires.

God has a perfect plan for each and every one of us. This plan is the one most pleasing to Him, but it is also the plan which provides us with the greatest fulfillment. However, God also gives us the freedom to choose. We attempt to create a life of contentment and peace, but we soon learn that creating anything based on our own desires is meaningless - "a chasing after the wind." (Ecclesiastes 1:11).

We will only know God's perfect plan and obtain true fulfillment when we use our freedom to follow and seek Him with all our heart. (Jeremiah 29:13). Only then will God reveal Himself and provide new desires for us to pursue.

Psalm 37:4
"Delight yourself in the Lord and He will give you the desires of your heart."

What we create will always be driven by desire. We must therefore ensure that our desires are those provided by God. We must continue to draw near and allow Him to give us the desires of our heart.

OPPORTUNITY OF OUR WORDS

Everything we say has an effect on those around us. The effect is either positive or negative - very rarely are our words neutral.

Ephesians 4:29

"Do not let any unwholesome talk come out of your mouths, but only what is helpful for building others up according to their needs, that it may benefit those who listen."

This means that every time we speak, we have the opportunity to encourage - an opportunity to minister. With just a few moments of our time and very little effort, we have the opportunity to brighten someone's day, to lighten the load they may be carrying, and possibly draw them closer to God. This precious opportunity must not be taken lightly.

Proverbs 18:13

"He who answers before listening - that is his folly and his shame."

Before we speak, we must listen very carefully. What is the real question? What are the real needs? We may only be allowed a few words - make sure they will be useful: "The heart of the righteous weighs its answers, but the mouth of the wicked gushes evil." (Proverbs 15:28).

Our words can be a very effective source of encouragement, but they can also be used to cause great harm. "Like a madman shooting firebrands or deadly arrows is a man who deceives his neighbor and says, 'I was only joking!'" (Proverbs 26:18-19). Sarcastic and joking words are "deadly arrows" which are never useful for "building others up." Over time, this mode of communication will destroy a relationship.

Our words are a powerful gift. Let's honor our Heavenly Father by effectively using this gift to encourage. Let's speak so that those who listen may benefit and be built up. Let's not squander the opportunity of our words!

FORGIVE BY GOD'S STANDARD

It seems like sooner or later, everyone gets mistreated, stepped on, lied to, or just plain hurt. Many times the actions against us are unintentional, but other times they can be extremely malicious. When this happens, it's as if someone opened our pack and added a hundred pound weight. Every area of our life seems to become heavy.

Some would advise that good old fashioned revenge is the best answer. They say we won't be rid of the weight until we "get even." Others advise to simply do nothing and learn to adjust to the added weight. Our walk would be greatly slowed, but at least no one else would suffer...or would they? When we carry an unnecessary burden, everyone around us becomes weighed down.

Colossians 3:13

"Bear with each other and forgive whatever grievances you may have against one another. Forgive as the Lord forgave you."

God's "advice" is to forgive. Our sins are forgiven through faith in Jesus Christ - plus nothing. But a saving faith is one which understands the grace of salvation and is then compelled to forgive others. We don't forgive because someone deserves or has earned our forgiveness - we should not even require an admission of guilt - we forgive one another simply because God first forgave us.

When we forgive, we must follow God's example by making the forgiveness complete. "For I will forgive their wickedness and will remember their sins no more." (Hebrews 8:12). When we forgive, we must not place conditions on the relationship by holding a grudge - or holding back our love. When God forgives, it's as if the sin never happened!

There WILL be times when we feel trampled. When we do, let's not follow the "advice" of the world. Every potential burden is an opportunity to grow closer to our Heavenly Father and to share His love with others. Let's follow the commands of God's Word. Let's forgive - and forgive by God's standard.

WHAT IT MEANS TO FORGIVE

In the message, "Forgive By God's Standard," we saw that forgiveness must be without condition and must be complete: "I will remember their sins no more." (Hebrews 8:12). But what does it really mean to forgive by God's standard?

Ephesians 4:31-32

"Get rid of all bitterness, rage and anger, brawling and slander, along with every form of malice. Be kind and compassionate to one another, forgiving each other, just as in Christ God forgave you."

As with every other issue in our Christian walk, forgiveness is a condition of the heart. We are commanded to forgive those who wrong us - whether or not they repent or even ask for our forgiveness. We forgive others because we understand the forgiveness given to us through the death of Jesus Christ: "While we were still sinners, Christ died for us." (Romans 5:8). By focusing on the magnitude of our sin and Christ's forgiveness, we will be better able to forgive the transgressions of others toward us. (Matthew 18:23-35).

Forgiveness means we cancel the emotional debt. It means we are able to love the other person and earnestly pray for blessings in their life. When we have forgiven, we are able to think about the other person without our insides becoming twisted. We should be able to pray for an increase in their ministry or business, more peace in their family life, and a closer relationship with Jesus Christ. And if the Holy Spirit so leads, we must be prepared to obediently follow toward complete restoration.

However, forgiveness is defined by the heart. Not all relationships can, nor even should, be restored to the previous condition (particularly in the absence of repentance). Forgiveness does not necessarily mean we trust or become "best friends" with someone who has caused us pain. We are responsible to use good judgement - but our decisions must be made without anger in our heart. For example, my forgiveness of a child abuser does not require me to leave my children in their care - but it requires that I love them and continue to pray for them without anger.

It's unfortunate, but most of us are carrying some bitterness and anger toward another person today. These emotions should not continue in the heart of a child of God - and the only road to release them is through forgiveness. Let's ask God to purify our heart...and honor Him by showing the world what it means to forgive.

STEP OF FAITH

The story of Peter walking on the water with Jesus provides us with a wonderful lesson on faith.

Matthew 14:28-29

"'Lord, if it's You,' Peter replied, 'tell me to come to You on the water.' 'Come,' He said. Then Peter got down out of the boat, walked on the water and came toward Jesus."

When Peter stepped onto the water, there was nothing within his physical senses which told him the water would hold. The waves were rolling and the wind was blowing - and he certainly had many past experiences telling him that heavy objects sink in water.

However, Peter KNEW Jesus. He had spent time with Jesus - he had walked with Him, talked with Him, and prayed with Him. Peter knew the face of Jesus and he knew His voice. He knew that if Jesus said "Come," He would also provide a way. Jesus made the water solid, but only where Peter stepped - and only after he stepped out in faith.

The step of faith is needed for any situation which requires a solution beyond what our physical senses can understand. "Now faith is being sure of what we hope for and certain of what we do not see." (Hebrews 11:1). The step of faith may be related to finances, a job, or ministry opportunities. But it may also be related to raising children, challenges at school, that troubling coworker - or anything else which requires us to operate outside the comfort of the boat.

Is God calling you out of the boat today? We must spend quality time with our Lord so we can recognize His voice, but when God says "Come," our only response is to step. Our past experiences may scream that it's not possible and we may not see any solid ground ahead, but we must trust that the One who called will provide the solid foundation with every step we take - with each and every step of faith!

FOCUSED ON JESUS

Peter demonstrated incredible faith as he stepped out of the boat and walked on the water toward Jesus. His faith in Jesus allowed him to look past his own understanding of the situation and trust the One who was calling. However, this pillar of faith, who would later heal the sick and fearlessly preach the Gospel, also had some of the same weaknesses you and I face every day.

Peter had a temper which caused him to act in anger as he cut off a soldier's ear while in the garden with Jesus. (John 18:10). His fear of persecution caused him to deny Jesus three times (Luke 22:56-62), and while on the water, Peter showed he was susceptible to losing his focus.

Matthew 14:30
> *"But when he (Peter) saw the wind, he was afraid and, beginning to sink, cried out, 'Lord, save me!'"*

Let's not be too hard on Peter - remember, no one else even left the boat! Peter stepped out of the boat and took several steps on top of the water!! But then he lost his focus.

Peter began to sink when he took his eyes off Jesus. Peter was in the middle of an awesome display of God's power and yet he "saw the wind." No one can actually see wind - we only see the effects of wind. Peter began to look around at the world and not at the One who created the world: "Let us fix our eyes on Jesus, the author and perfecter of our faith." (Hebrews 12:2).

There are times when we clearly see God's hand at work. Our eyes become focused on Jesus, His peace fills our life, and the foundation under our feet feels solid and secure. However, it's usually not long before the wind begins to blow, the waves rise up, and we feel that sinking feeling.

When this happens (and it will), don't despair - for this is also part of God's wonderful plan. As we are sinking, He always offers an invitation to know Him better - to KNOW He will always be there when we cry out "Lord, save me!" The walk of faith cannot be accomplished in our own strength. With each step we must recommit to trusting - recommit to taking our eyes off the world and keeping them focused on Jesus.

HEAR THE CALL

When Peter responded to Jesus' call to walk on the water, Jesus provided the firm foundation under Peter's feet as he stepped. Peter had no special gift of water walking - he simply heard the call and obeyed. If Peter would have sailed the next day - even to the exact same spot - and stepped out of the boat without being called, he would have sunk like a rock. All of Peter's mighty faith would not have kept him on top of the water for even a fraction of a second. Peter's "success" on the water was not due as much to his faith as it was to hearing the call of Jesus.

John 10:27

"My sheep listen to My voice; I know them, and they follow Me."

My family and I visited a water park last week. Our four-year-old daughter climbed one of those multi-level slides with ramps, tunnels, and water cannons. When she was near the top, she started yelling "Hi Dad!!" There must have been over 100 screaming kids surrounding this one small voice, but my ears were "tuned" and her voice jumped out as if it was the only sound on a quiet morning. Even though I couldn't see her, I stood up and started to wave. After a few moments, I managed to see her beaming face waving back. My daughter and I spend lots of time together - I KNOW her voice.

How often do we set aside time to listen to the voice of our Heavenly Father? If we only occasionally listen, will we even recognize His voice when He calls? We must not wait until the crisis of a storm. If we haven't learned to filter out the competing noises of the world, God's call will be lost in the crashing waves.

We must spend time away from the "noise" where we can be alone with God and learn to recognize His voice. We must establish times of quiet to read His Word and talk with Him in prayer. "Sanctify them by the truth; Your Word is truth." (John 17:17). Spending time in the Word of God can set us apart from the distractions of the world. By meditating on His truth and praying for understanding, we refine our Spiritual filter. When we enter the storm, there may be 100 competing voices, but a properly tuned filter will allow only a single voice to pass.

Let's develop the discipline of listening along with the Spiritual ability to filter and recognize the voice of our Lord. Our faith will be enough to respond - strong enough to step - but we first must have the ability to hear the call.

MEET THEM WHERE THEY ARE

This is the fourth message in a series about Peter answering the call to walk with Jesus on the water.

In the first message, "Step of Faith," we saw Peter hear the call of Jesus and step onto the water - even though he had no idea how the water would hold. We were encouraged that when Jesus calls, we are to trust He will provide a way to follow.

In the second message, "Focused on Jesus," we saw Peter look at the waves and begin to sink. We were reminded to always keep our eyes on Jesus and not on the storm. The third message, "Hear The Call," dealt with the importance of spending time with God so we can recognize His voice and filter out the competing noise when He calls.

Today, we look at the example Jesus gave in ministering to one another. When Peter began to sink, he cried out to Jesus: "Lord, save me!" (Matthew 14:30).

Matthew 14:31-33
> *"Immediately Jesus reached out His hand and caught him. 'You of little faith,' He said, 'why did you doubt?' And when they climbed into the boat, the wind died down. Then those who were in the boat worshiped Him, saying, 'Truly You are the Son of God.'"*

Jesus' words to Peter might seem a little harsh. After all, Peter had stepped onto the water while the other disciples remained in the boat. But Peter needed to be encouraged in what true faith could accomplish. God had great plans for Peter - so Jesus ministered to Peter's doubts and fears as He met him on the water.

Jesus then climbed in the boat with the other disciples. Rather than chastising them for their lack of faith, He simply allowed them to worship. These disciples had failed to understand and needed to spend time just loving and worshiping their Lord. Jesus ministered to these disciples as He met them in the boat.

Every day God places people in our life who need the encouragement we have to offer. None of us know all the answers, but we each can play a part to help others along the way. Let's look for the specific needs of those who cross our path and encourage with Biblical truth at every opportunity. Whether on the water or in the boat, we must minister as we meet them where they are.

FULL MEASURE OF OUR HEART

When God gave the Law to Moses, He specified rules for worship and rules for how people should treat one another. When Jesus was asked to state the most important commandment, He replied: "Love the Lord your God will all your heart and with all your soul and with all your mind and with all your strength." (Mark 12:30). At another point in His ministry, Jesus taught that the Law and the Prophets are summed up as you "do to others what you would have them do to you." (Matthew 7:12).

God demands honesty in His people. "You must have accurate and honest weights and measures. For the Lord detests anyone who deals dishonestly." (Deuteronomy 25:15-16). Jesus emphasized the use of fair measurement standards as He taught His disciples.

Luke 6:38
"Give, and it will be given to you. A good measure, pressed down, shaken together and running over, will be poured into your lap. For with the measure you use, it will be measured to you."

Jesus Christ died for the forgiveness of our sins so we might receive "the blessing given to Abraham." (Galatians 3:14). This blessing includes the right to be called children of God and the inheritance of eternal life, but it also extends to our days on earth as we receive the blessings of true joy, peace, and contentment.

It should not be surprising that the measure of blessing we receive from God is directly related to the measure we use to give unto Him. This measure has little to do with the amount of our financial gifts: "To obey is better than sacrifice and to heed is better than the fat of rams." (1 Samuel 15:22). We can't "purchase" our blessings. Rather, our measure unto God is our worship and obedience. It is our desire to walk every moment of our day in His presence and praise Him with every breath.

Our dealings with God become dishonest and deceitful when we expect a full measure of His blessing of peace, His blessing of clear direction, or even His blessing of assurance, and yet cheat Him with every measure we return. There is only one way to receive the full measure of God's blessing. We must first praise Him and give Him the full measure of our worship - we must follow wherever He leads and bless Him with the full measure of our heart.

THE LOVE OF CHRIST

"In the beginning God created the heavens and the earth." (Genesis 1:1). And in the beginning, God's plan of Salvation through Jesus was established. "For God so loved the world..." (John 3:16). Even though He knew we would rebel - even though He knew we would turn our backs and worship other gods - even though He knew we would live as slaves to our sinful nature - He created us and provided a way to return to Him through faith in Jesus Christ.

Ephesians 3:17-19

"And I pray that you, being rooted and established in love, may have power, together with all the saints, to grasp how wide and long and high and deep is the love of Christ, and to know this love that surpasses knowledge."

Paul's prayer is that we would begin to comprehend the magnitude of God's love for us - the magnitude of love demonstrated at the cross. "But God demonstrates His own love for us in this: While we were still sinners, Christ died for us." (Romans 5:8).

"When I think of the wisdom and scope of God's plan, I fall to my knees and pray." (Ephesians 3:14 NLT). It's only as we begin to grasp the extent of this love that we are able to live as we were created to live - conformed to the likeness of Christ (Romans 8:29). It's only through the belief and understanding of this love that we can truly praise and worship with grateful hearts - that we can serve with overflowing thankfulness - that we can truly forgive and love one another. "As I have loved you, so you must love one another." (John 13:34).

Heavenly Father, we pray that You would grant us an understanding of Your love - the love which You demonstrated through Jesus. We pray that this understanding would cause us to love You in return. We pray that our love for You would be shown through our worship, our service, and our love for others. Father, we ask that today, You would open our eyes to the love of Christ.

HOLD ME

When a young child wants to be held, they simply reach up and say: "Hold me Daddy!" As he looks down, no loving father evaluates the child to determine if they deserve to be held, or sends the child away to earn affection. A loving father picks up the child and holds them with no words even being required. When asked, a loving father will say moments like this are his greatest joy!

Matthew 18:3

"I tell you the truth, unless you change and become like little children, you will never enter the kingdom of heaven."

Our Heavenly Father loves us very much. He wants us to come to Him with outstretched arms...He wants to pick us up and hold us tight. Moments like this are His greatest joy! And yet, we spend our days trying to make ourselves acceptable - trying to earn our Father's affection.

In the eye's of God, we all have the understanding and the abilities of a child. We pour our hearts into projects thinking they are vitally important to God's work. We try to please Him as we say, "Daddy, look what I made You!" But our best efforts are as grade school pencil holders and disfigured flower pots.

Our Father takes these gifts, places them on the shelf, smiles, and shakes His head wishing we would understand. There's much work that needs to be accomplished for the Kingdom of God, but none more important than loving and being loved by Daddy. "'The most important one,' answered Jesus, 'is this: Hear O Israel, the Lord your God is one. Love the Lord your God with all your heart...'" (Mark 12:29-30).

Yes, we must clean our room, take out the trash, and treat others nice on the playground - but at the end of the day, we must all reach up with empty arms and say: I love You Daddy - hold me!

RIGHT WHERE HE WANTS US

Joseph's brothers developed a jealous hatred for him because their father "loved Joseph more than any of his other sons." (Genesis 37:3). The hatred was intensified when Joseph told his brothers some dreams about them bowing down to him (Genesis 37:5-9). The brothers plotted to kill Joseph but instead sold him into slavery.

Joseph was taken to Egypt and sold to Potiphar who was the captain of the guard for Pharaoh. After a short time, Joseph was falsely accused by Potiphar's wife and thrown in jail. Joseph could really have felt sorry for himself - things were not going very well! Only a short time before, Joseph's path in life had seemed well established - he knew where he was going and it brought him great joy. Now, in prison, he had truly hit bottom.

Genesis 39:20-22

"But while Joseph was there in the prison, the Lord was with him; He showed him kindness and granted him favor in the eyes of the prison warden. So the warden put Joseph in charge of all those held in the prison, and he was made responsible for all that was done there."

While in jail, Joseph interpreted dreams for some of Pharaoh's officials (Genesis 40) and was then called to interpret a dream for Pharaoh. This opportunity placed Joseph in a position of great responsibility. "So Pharaoh said to Joseph, 'I hereby put you in charge of the whole land of Egypt.'" (Genesis 41:41). It was God's plan to place Joseph in a position to save many lives - including the lives of his father and brothers (Genesis 42-48).

Through all his trials, Joseph never complained. He trusted God during the worst of times and continually looked for the good - even though he didn't understand God's plan until many years of hardship had passed.

No matter what this day brings, we must keep looking for God's good. It may truly feel as if we're in a prison with no way of escape - but if we are walking in the light of Jesus, we must trust that we are right where He wants us!

INDEX OF SCRIPTURE REFERENCES

INDEX OF SCRIPTURE REFERENCES

INDEX OF SCRIPTURE REFERENCES